Lines and Circles
A Celebration
of Santa Fe Families

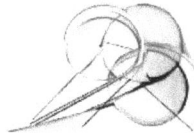

Lines and Circles
A Celebration
of Santa Fe Families

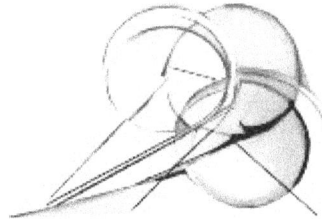

edited by
Valerie Martínez
Santa Fe Poet Laureate and Project Director

SUNSTONE
PRESS

SANTA FE

"Lines and Circles"
was a Project of the Santa Fe Arts Commission Poet Laureate Program (2008–2010)

Exhibition January–March 2010
Santa Fe Arts Commission Community Gallery
Santa Fe, New Mexic

Sunstone books may be purchased for educational, business, or sales promotional use.
For information please write: Special Markets Department, Sunstone Press,
P.O. Box 2321, Santa Fe, New Mexico 87504-2321.

Book and Cover design ›Vicki Ahl
Body typeface ›CG Omega
Printed on acid free paper

Library of Congress Cataloging-in-Publication Data

Martínez, Valerie, 1951-
  Lines and circles : a celebration of Santa Fe families / edited by
Valerie Martínez.
    p. cm.
  ISBN 978-0-86534-746-5 (softcover : alk. paper)
  1. Santa Fe (N.M.)--Biography. 2. Santa Fe (N.M.)--Genealogy.
3. Santa Fe (N.M.)--Social life and customs. 4. Santa Fe
(N.M.)--Intellectual life. I. Title.
  F804.S253A263 2010date
  978.9'56--dc22

                              2009046950

Published in

WWW.SUNSTONEPRESS.COM
SUNSTONE PRESS / POST OFFICE BOX 2321 / SANTA FE, NM 87504-2321 /USA
(505) 988-4418 / ORDERS ONLY (800) 243-5644 / FAX (505) 988-1025

Lines and Circles
A Celebration
of Santa Fe Families

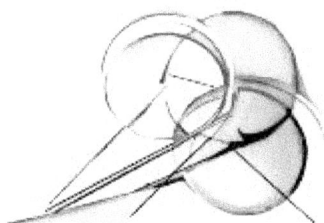

Contents

Acknowledgments

rateful acknowledgement is made to the following organizations and individuals who made the Lines and Circles Project possible: Mayor David Coss and the City of Santa Fe; Sabrina Pratt and the City of Santa Fe Arts Commission; the Lannan Foundation; the Santa Fe Literary Education Endowment at the Santa Fe Community Foundation; First National Bank of Santa Fe; Rod Lambert and the Santa Fe Arts Commission Community Gallery; Littleglobe, Inc; Maurice Bonal, Libby Dover, and the staff of the Santa Fe 400th Anniversary Commemoration; Maris Segal and Ken Ashby of Prosody Creative Services, Inc; James Clois Smith, Jr. and the staff of Sunstone Press; College of Santa Fe; Marilyn Batts; Lauren Camp; Agustin Carmona; Leland Chapin; Jennifer Dann; Jason Jaacks; Chris Jonas; Ilana Kirshbaum; Tom Maguire; Gary Myers; Zevin Polzin; Seth Roffman; Paul Resnick; Shelle Sánchez; Molly Sturges, and Eileen Torpey.

With warmest thanks to the Lines and Circles families whose beautiful and hard work made this book possible.

Preface

*I*n 2005, the city of Santa Fe appointed its first poet laureate and began an exciting series of poetry programs. They have resulted in heightened awareness of the literary arts and a spreading of the joy of poetry in our community. The honorary position is given to a person who has established a reputation in the world of poetry and embraces the opportunity to engage in civic discourse. During the two-year appointment, each poet laureate has a ceremonial role, reading at important community events. The poet also uses his or her creativity in introducing poetry to the community in innovative ways.

Some of the objectives for the program are to:

Enhance the literary arts presence in Santa Fe,
Create a focal point for the expression of Santa Fe's culture through the
    literary arts,
Provide a forum for cross pollination of art forms,
Celebrate the spirit of the people and the special qualities of our city,
Create a unique program that will become a model for other cities, and
Create, over a period of time, a body of work that commemorates the life
    of our city.

Included in the philosophy of our program is the idea that over the course of the two years the poet should nourish his or her own personal growth and interests, concurrent with an educational outreach initiative. Valerie Martínez is our second poet laureate, serving in that capacity from March 2008 through March 2010. The selection committee that recommended her appointment found her proposed education program, *Lines and Circles*, to be particularly thoughtful and compelling, and it has developed into a very meaningful experience for the participants. The project mixes the literary arts with the visual arts, celebrates history and the unique people of our city, and provides opportunities for the public to learn, meeting all of our program objectives.

Poet Laureate Valerie Martínez's community project is outstanding in its deep engagement with Santa Fe families. Readers of this book will find that her work is a model for community-based projects. It has resulted in the gathering of community members to prepare work that reflects the lives of the dozen families and thereby Santa Fe at-large. The Arts Commission is extremely proud of this project, which helps us to meet our goal of creating access to the arts for Santa Feans.

—Sabrina Pratt, Executive Director
City of Santa Fe Arts Commission

Thanks to a generous donor, the Santa Fe Literary Education Endowment at the Santa Fe Community Foundation was established to support and ensure the longevity of the Poet Laureate Program. Contributions are welcomed and may be sent to the Foundation at P.O. Box 1827, Santa Fe, New Mexico 87504–1827.

The Lines and Circles Families Project: Bringing Santa Fe Together Across the Generations

by
Valerie Martínez,
Poet Laureate 2008–2010, Project Director

I hope this book makes you believe in the future of Santa Fe as much as I do. The families you'll read about in these pages are a testament not only to city history but the promise of days to come. The future, of course, rests upon the beautiful, complex, rich and contentious past of this place, the capital city of New Mexico. All places worth living in, I believe, are complicated. So are their people. While many tout the landscape of Santa Fe as the city's richest asset, the truth is that the people of Santa Fe, those that are here to stay, are its gold. They know its past and present and they cut, carve, and burnish its future. Their family lines extend far into the past and the circles they trace, day to day in this city, fashion the shimmering design that is the lifeblood of our community.

It has been my honor and pleasure to serve as Santa Fe's second Poet Laureate. I have participated in over forty public readings and events over my two-year tenure, and I have had the opportunity to meet and mingle with a wide range of Santa Fe residents—in schools, senior centers, libraries, museums, at swearings-in, conferences, gala events, with elementary school students, teenagers, college students, families, city elders, and others. Santa Feans, everywhere, have shared their perspectives, and I have learned much about what we love about our city and how we want it to change. Each and every encounter has deepened my experience and knowledge of this place, and I have come to love my hometown and its complicated history and reality even more profoundly than before.

Perhaps my deepest learning has come as a result of the *Lines and Circles* project—the educational/outreach/community program I created as Poet Laureate, and the subject of this book. For over a year and a half, I have worked closely with three generations of eleven Santa Fe families who have created unique family "works" that premiered, with this book, in the exhibition entitled *Lines and Circles: A Celebration of Santa Fe Families* on January 15, 2010. As you read these pages, you too will come to know not only the stories of these families but the "story" of Santa Fe life from past to present, told through the eyes of its residents. In this, you will learn much about what life *was* and *is* like for the Santa Feans who love their city and are deeply invested in its welfare.

The goal of the *Lines and Circles* project was to nurture and celebrate the Santa Fe community, encourage positive relationships within and between families, engage in meaningful community dialogue, and generate a body of art and poetry that commemorates city life. The project began in May of 2008 with a press release and flyer (in English and Spanish) that was distributed in the local media, community centers, libraries, schools and other public places. The project description read:

> "Santa Fe families with three generations living in the city are invited to participate in a community project entitled *Lines and Circles: A Celebration of Santa Fe Families*, led by Poet Laureate Valerie Martínez. This project gathers three generations of 10-15 individual Santa Fe families, each to compose/create a unique family "work" (story, short film, book, photograph, woodwork, quilt, sculpture, pottery, recording, mixed media piece, etc.). Any Santa Fe family is welcome; you need not be artists to participate. Families will work inter-generationally, with the Poet Laureate, and in company with each other. The works may reflect the family name, family history, or simply the intergenerational collaboration that happens during the project. Assistance for the families will come from local artists and artisans. Each work will also be accompanied by a poem. The poem may be authored by family members, by the family and the Poet Laureate writing together, or by the Poet Laureate, depending on the family's wishes. The finished pieces will constitute an exhibit entitled *Lines & Circles: A Celebration of Santa Fe Families* to be presented to the city in 2010."

By the autumn of 2008, sixteen families had come forward to participate in the project and thirteen continued until the end of the year. By the spring of 2009 eleven families were still involved. It's important to note that every family who came forward to be part of the project sincerely wanted to continue, but four families were challenged either by family loss, the complex logistics of working intergenerationally, or other reasons. In addition to the families in this book, I would like to thank the Simpson-Swentzell, Tsosie-Gaussoin, Gee, Lomahaftewa, and Maryol-Salis families for their interest and (in some cases) participation in the project though they were not able to continue to the end.

One of the many lessons of the project was the realization that it is very rare for generations of families to engage in sustained creative work together. Some families do *work* together and families *do* get together for celebrations, holidays, and other gatherings, but sustained creative work across generations is, sadly, a rare occurrence.

In addition, it's important to mention that no matter how wide the call for participating families, my efforts at reaching the widest range of families, and the broad diversity reflected in the finished project, the families do not and could not reflect all the kinds of families in Santa Fe. I wish it wasn't so. The good news is that a project like this could happen again and again, in the city, and cumulatively reflect more and more of the city's broad and deep family life.

The families who completed the project put in countless hours of work by brainstorming, designing, and building their family works. They completed long questionnaires and ancestral charts about their family members; they went through dozens of family photos to choose the ones shown here; they wrote poems; they worked with local artists; they burned up their phone lines and desktops and laptops answering messages from me. They received a little bit of money for their efforts and as much money and in-kind donations as the city and I could pull together (with thanks to our funders) to support the project. At the same time many local artists and artisans assisted the families, sometimes volunteering their precious time and expertise over the course of a year and a half. All to say, this project was more a labor of family and community love than anything else.

In this book, I have tried to preserve a strong sense of the words and work of the families themselves. You will see photos of the family works of art in progress (this book went to press before the works were completed).You will also see text, poems, translations and photos, contributed by family members, that I hope give you a sense of the many, individual "hands" that have touched this project.

And the project, in return, has touched all of us deeply. The families will tell you that in addition to creating and preserving an important family work that will stay with them for generations, they have come together, even more meaningfully, as families. We/they have also met, worked with, and become friends with families they didn't know, across the "invisible lines" that sometimes tend to separate us, as city residents. Together, we have also journeyed into the past with one another, learning the stories of eleven Santa Fe families that in many ways tell the story of Santa Fe.

This book is a gift from us to our city, to our fellow residents, and to anyone who wants to know more about those whose roots are deep in this beloved land. It is a testament to who we are, how we got here, and what we love and desire for this place that we call home.

—Valerie Martínez, 2009

Lines and Circles Families
Countries of Origin

*N*on-native ancestors of Lines and Circles Families migrated to Santa Fe from the following countries: Argentina, England/Great Britain, France, Germany, Hungary, Ireland, Italy, Lithuania, Mexico, Palestine, Portugal, Russia, Scotland, Spain, Sweden, and various states in the U.S.

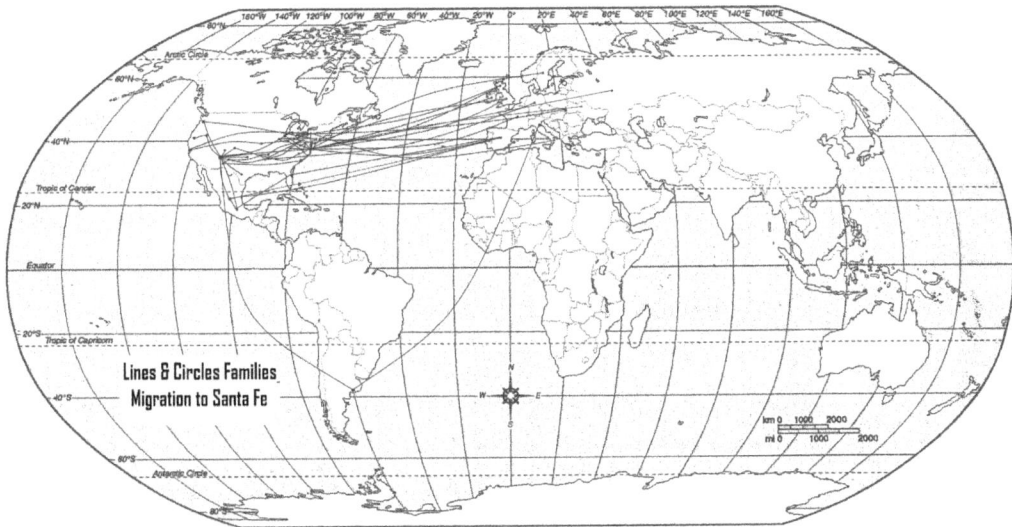

Lines & Circles Families
Migration to Santa Fe

Lines and Circles Families
Religions and Languages

Religions: Baptist, Presbyterian, Roman Catholic, Judaism (including Ashkenazic and *conversos*, Sephardic Jews), Pagan Spiritualist, Methodist, Agnostic, Shambala Buddhism, Episcopalian, Sun Worshipper, Quaker, Native American Church.

Languages: English, Russian, Spanish, Portuguese, Yiddish.

Lines and Circles Family
Homes in Santa Fe

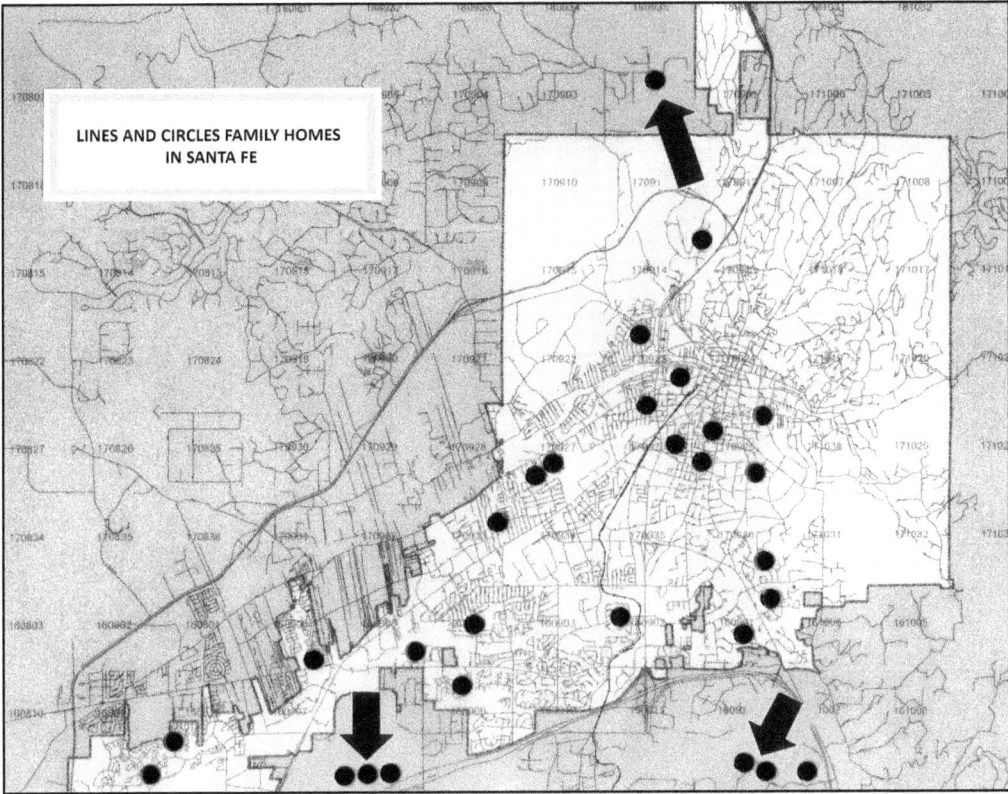

LINES AND CIRCLES FAMILY HOMES
IN SANTA FE

The
Akers Hunt Covelli
Family

Mary Louise Melton Akers
May 20, 1903 – December 28, 2007

The Akers Hunt Covelli Family

Participating Family Members and Ages

First Generation—Mary Louise Melton Akers (104, *in memoriam*)
Second Generation—Kathryn Ann Akers Hunt Flynn (73)
Third Generation—Charlotte Robyn Covelli-Hunt (54)
Fourth Generation—Delaney Camille Covelli (14)

Brief Family History
by Robyn Covelli-Hunt

*W*hen asked if our earliest ancestors were indigenous people of the Southwest I pondered, can an "Oakie" be considered indigenous? We are a family of predominantly white, Anglo-Saxon Protestants who migrated to Santa Fe or the surrounding area from the East—Virginia, Pennsylvania, Tennessee and Missouri, to name a few places—in the 1800s after leaving countries of origin including Germany, Italy, England, France and Scotland. From there family began to work their way to the Southwest and settled primarily in the panhandle regions of Oklahoma and Texas and in the neighboring state of New Mexico where many family members still live today.

The family was and is, in part, made up of farmers and educators, ranchers and ministers, government employees and well-meaning folk. Life began in New Mexico with homesteading coupled with the men running small grocery stores and gas stations; wives quilted and canned vegetables. A number of the women taught Bible study and wrote poetry. Some of us questioned authority even while presiding in positions of authority. Robert Hunt worked for NASA in the 1960's developing rocket trajectories to the moon; his daughter, Robyn, was arrested as a non-violent protester at Livermore Laboratory in California, the sister lab to Los Alamos. One family member made his mark, long ago, when he penned *The Wizard of Oz*. One grandfather built a church from the ground up and another boarded an immigrant ship as a boy with two sisters and one brother leaving Italy to join his father in New York.

Today three generations of women, Kathryn, Robyn and Delaney, ages 73 to 14, live in Santa Fe in the shadow of a prankster great grandmother, Mary Louise, who is represented in this project *in memoriam* and who passed away in Santa Fe in 2007 at the merry old age of 104. Mary Louise was famous, in her time, for making wise cracks, flirting, and nick-naming everyone she knew well, not the typical attributes of a preacher's wife.

Today, Mary Louise's daughter Kathryn (Kathy) Akers Hunt Flynn is Executive Director of the National New Deal Preservation Association and spends much of her time researching, writing, and publishing detailed information promoting the identification, documentation, preservation and education of people about New Deal visual and performing arts, literature, crafts, structures and environmental projects across the United States. She has published two books, *Treasures on New Mexico Trails: Discover New Deal Art and Architecture* (Sunstone Press, 1995) and *The New Deal: A 75th Anniversary Celebration* (Gibbs Smith, 2008). Daughter Robyn Covelli-Hunt is Assistant to the Program Director of the Santa Fe Community Infant Program which provides mental health services to infants and toddlers in Santa Fe County at Las Cumbres Community Services; she is also a writer whose poetry has appeared in a number of anthologies. Her daughter, Delaney Covelli, is a high school student at Santa Fe High. She enjoys music, dance, graphic design and her many, many close friends.

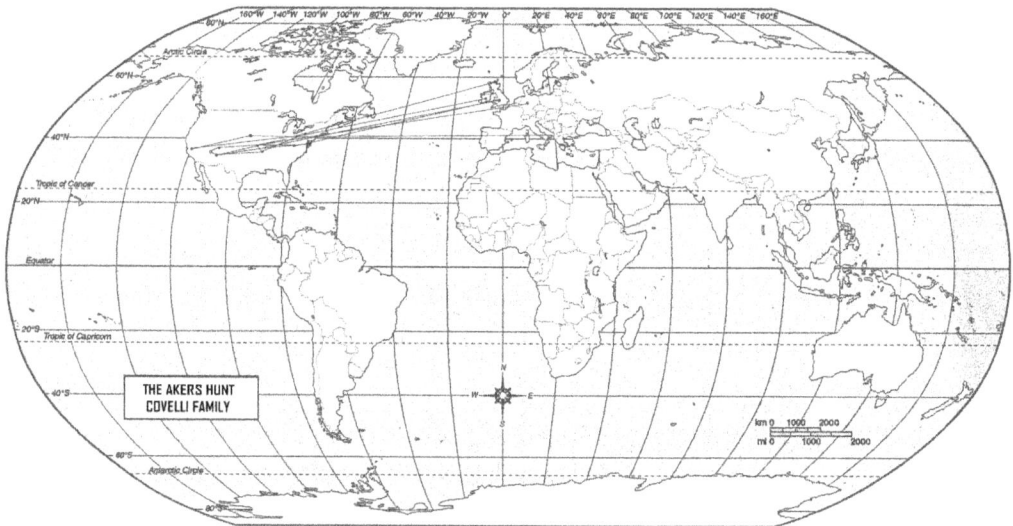

THE AKERS HUNT COVELLI FAMILY

Family Traditions

Late night church services on Christmas Eve and then cookies and milk left out for Santa Claus. We enjoy the Canyon Road Farolito Walk, also on Christmas Eve., and often place farolitos on our front walks as well. Past traditions that are, unfortunately, passing away include making and canning jam, and embroidering tablecloths for wedding gifts.

Family Recipes

Cinnamon rolls. Oatmeal with apples and raisins.

Family Heirlooms

A wedding dress and christening gown on the Akers side of the family. Family Bibles.

What We Love About Santa Fe

The plaza. The wide, inspiring blue sky. The spirituality that exists in many shapes and sizes.

Our Greatest Hopes for Our Family

We hope that Delaney will carry on the family legacy of the written word, stay politically and socially aware and outspoken; that she will strive as her mother, grandmother, and great grandparents have, before her, to always work toward bettering the community around her, from within her immediate home out into the wider world.

The Akers Hunt Covelli Family Today

Lineage Maker
by
Robyn Covelli-Hunt
for my daughter, Delaney

To see my grandmother's christening gown
on the body of our tiny daughter is to drink from its linen bowl
one broad sip at a time.
She beams up from the bed, baby belle
in a puddle of cloth. She bequeaths us her smile
in this thinning attire
with a hem reinforced to outlive us.

Our girl, not yet princess, sits
in this precious drape and hears the whispers
of those who crawled inside this tent before her.
I wore this dress and my mother wore it.
We were gathered like white tuberoses in our parents' arms
for submersion into certain communion.

What a fine sturdy sail for the crossing, ships rocking
from Europe to these United States. Family settling
in Missouri, Tennessee, Kentucky, and New York.
Then on across counties dry of spirit to picture windmills, lodge cattle,
where one homestead porch leans up against another
and hard working cousins can rest with iced tea clinking,
eating homegrown.

This dress smelling of cedar wrapped in tissue in a yellowing box
is testament to the mothers and fathers who came before—
lineage maker sewn by a friend is map of the family feminine
Oakies and Texans on a trajectory for the future where they will
deliver mail, stretch quilt frames, and teach—
crossing the Rio Grande landscape first on horses and then
with speedometers in reliable cars on their way westward to Santa Fe.

Boys, not quite men, will sweep the family grocery store floor
each evening. Wash their hands, wrists, and arms up to the elbows
then sit down together for prayer. They will gobble up enchiladas or
potpies, okra fried in corn meal, and retire to evening's recline.
Poppie will cease typing his sermons, and Grammie will sit
at the maple vanity braiding her thin hair before bedtime.

Whole generations of pretty girls will persevere, singing,
endless days of dry wind, cross stitch, and Protestant hymns.
Bobby pins and hairnets in the chestnut hair of aunts and mothersgrandmothers
and cousins settling in the pews in front of them.
Fathers, uncles, and big brothers trading cowboy hats and bolo ties
for tie tacks and cuff links. Dapper gents growing
into leisure suits and straw hats.

And all of this recorded in Little Mother Cleo's letters stored
in dresser drawers and dark, receptive cubby holes of antique desks.
All the words of God's galloping daughters and their visions
history's cursive penmanship grown wobbly like leaning cattle fences
secured again and again, like a necessary hem.

One day my daughter will pour her baby into this crinoline waterfall
and history will hitch itself to her shutter finger.

It will be written.

The Akers Hunt Covelli Family

William **AKERS**, 17th Century
New Jersey

Simon Akers, NJ, d. 1722
m. "Mary"

Robert Akers, b. 1703, NJ
m. **Sarah** , b. 1706

William Akers, b. 1730 VA
m. **Elizabeth Martye**, PA

John Akers, b. 1763 VA
m. **Agnes Bryan**

George Akers, b. 1787 VA
m. **Nancy Davis**

Simon Peter Akers
m. **Catherine Elizabeth
Llewellyn** b. 1831

Charles Edward Akers,
b. 1863 MO m
Cleo Avice Earl, b. 1876 MO

Homer Clifford Akers,
b. 1903 MO
m. **Mary Louise Melton** in
1930

Kathryn Ann Akers. b 1936 TX
m. **Robert Weldon Hunt**
Children: Charlotte Robyn, Shawna
Lynne, Robert Weldon

Charlotte Robyn Hunt,
b. 1956 TX
m. **Robert Patrick COVELLI**
Children: **Delaney Camille Covelli**,
b. 1995, Santa Fe (Half-Brother Tasio
Pieri)

Hamilton **HUNT**, b. 1844 MO
m. **Mary Elizabeth Hurley**
b. 1842 TN

Alonzo Hamilton Hunt b. 1892 TX
m. **Mary (Mollie) Elefair Martin**,
b. 1869 TX

Malcolm Garrett Hunt
b. 1912 TX m.
Audrey Bernice Cayton
b. 1911 TX

Robert Weldon Hunt.
b. 1935, Portales, NM
m. **Kathryn Ann Akers**
b. 1936 TX
Children: Charlotte Robyn, Shawna Lynne,
Robert Weldon

Charlotte Robyn Hunt, b. 1956 TX
m. **Robert Patrick COVELLI**
Children: **Delaney Camille Covelli**
b. 1995, Santa Fe
(Tasio Pieri , half-brother)

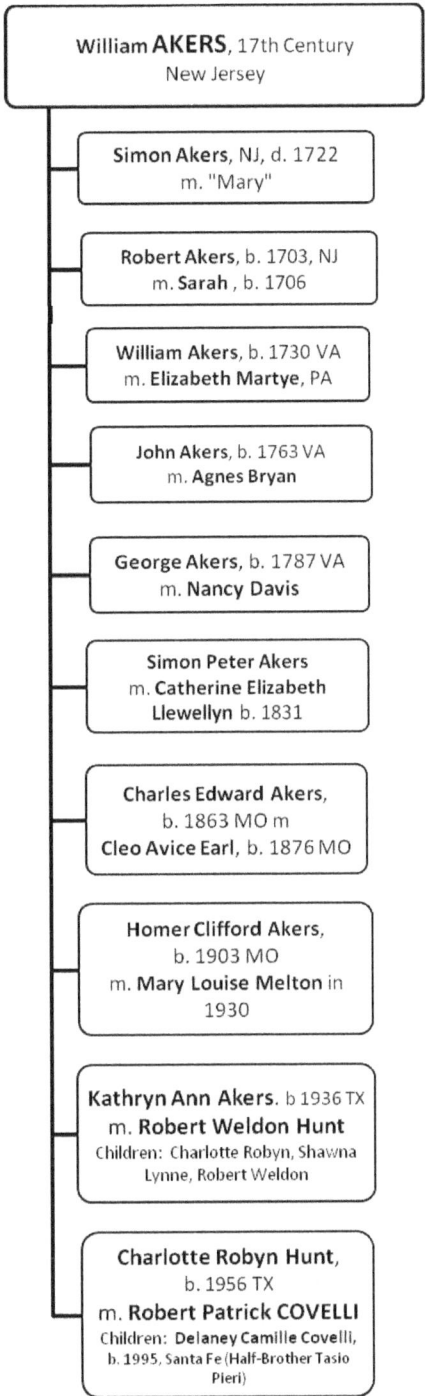

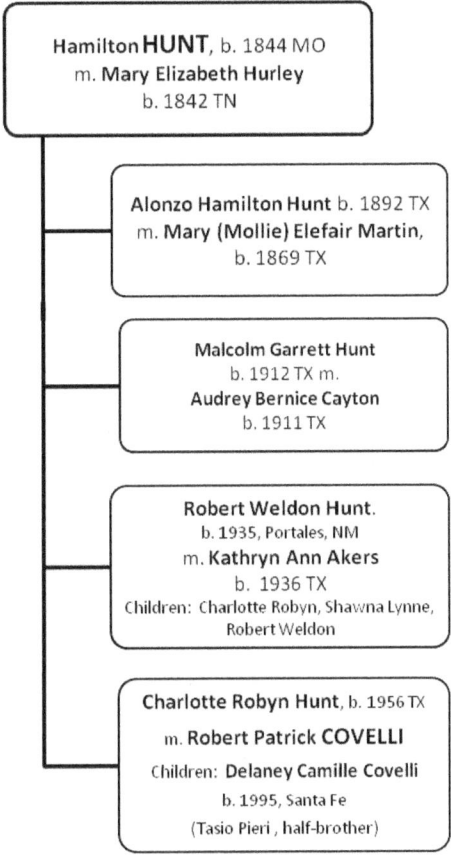

THE AKERS
HUNT COVELLI FAMILY

The Carmona Family

María with her children, Marisela and Heriberto, Zacatecas, Mexico, early 1990s.

The Carmona Family

Participating Family Members and Ages

First Generation—María Dominguez de Carmona (40); Agustín Carmona (38)
Second Generation—Marisela Dominguez (24), Heriberto Dominguez (22), Richard Dominguez (11), Jessica Carmona (5)
Third Generation—Xavier Soto Carrillo (4), Ernesto Orlando Tafoya (2), Lucas Damian Tafoya (1)

Brief Family History
as told by
María Dominguez de Carmona

"I came to Santa Fe in 1990. It was about realizing a dream. I wanted something better for my kids, better schools, better opportunities. I left my two young children and traveled north (from Zacatecas) without them. At first I didn't want to come; but my Mom told me she would take care of my kids until I could find work.

Me and my friend Concha arrived in Juarez. I got a job making corn and flour tortillas. After paying rent and food we managed to save 170 dollars. My friend found someone named "Mario" who said he could help us. The day we decided to cross it was 11 p.m. and we crossed the river and the border. We were under the bridge. When the border patrol came one way we rolled and crawled the other way. We got on the train at 5 a.m. We had to get on while it was moving. When I think back now, I could have lost my legs, arms. We didn't have coats and it was so cold.

We got off the train at 11 a.m. at Socorro. I was covered with bruises. We walked a couple of miles through the fields. We washed in the river. We had brought plastic bags with deodorant, soap and a change of clothes. We were so hungry. I remember we went to Allsups and bought food to make sandwiches outside. The next day we got a lift to Los Lunas and then rides to Albuquerque and Santa Fe.

We finally got to a 7-11 on Cerrillos Road. That was how we arrived. I just started walking and trying to find a job. I got lost and spoke to some Mexican men who were changing the windows on a house. One of them knocked on the door and told Mrs. Agnes Trujillo that I was his niece and could I clear up after they had finished. I did and she offered to give me work the following week. I earned just enough money to pay for a motel room, so I used to eat apples from her garden. I remember living once for a full week on apples and nothing else.

Finally I told Mrs. Trujillo that I had no money to eat. She invited me to live at her house. I lived with her for six months. She didn't just open her door to me; she opened her heart. Mrs Trujillo called her friends and set me up with work. I saved 700 dollars, my first savings to send to my mother for my children. I gave this to a man who promised to give it to my family but he stole it. When I look back, I feel frightened now for what I did then. I was just following a dream and nothing else seemed important; even dying didn't seem important.

I wanted to help my children, my mother and my family. I made it; despite all the difficulties. It's not about getting here; it's about making a life once you get here. I feel I'm so lucky to be here. I feel as though I am home. Santa Fe is my home."

Note: Agnes Trujillo is the mother of Exilda Trujillo Martínez, see the Martínez Ridgley Family.

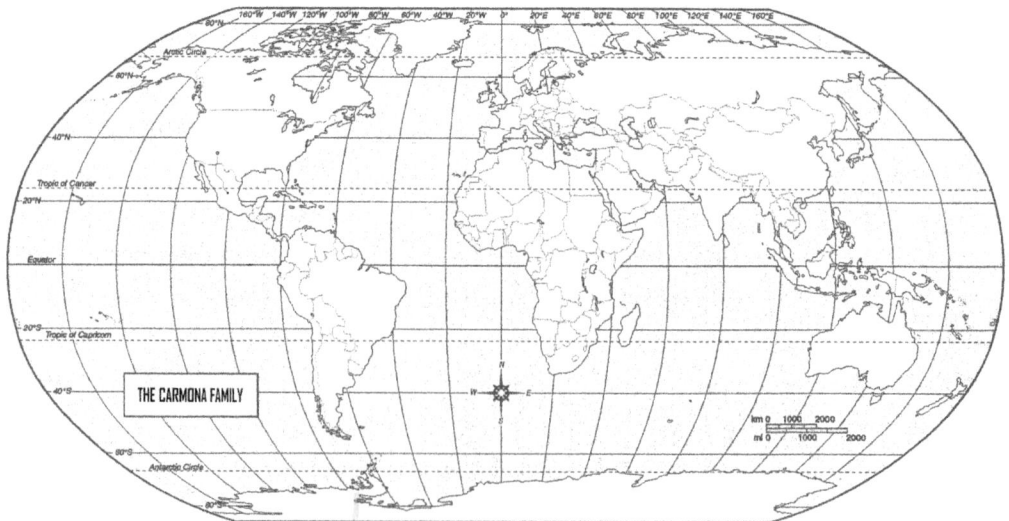

THE CARMONA FAMILY

Family Traditions

os juntamos para Navidad, Año nuevo y también para cada cumpleaños. También adoptamos nuevas tradiciones de este país como el día de acción de gracias, 4 de Julio, tiempo de Pascua, día del amor, día de San Patricio. Cuando mis hermanos y yo estabamos creciendo les teniamos que hablar de *usted* a nuestras mayores, no de *tu* como ahora. También, cuando encontran abuelos, padres, padrinos teniamos que besar la mano al saludarlos, eso era una forma de respeto. Si se acostumbra que si tienes un niño baron siempre le quieres poner como su papa o como su abuelito, por ejemplo Agustin se llama como mi abuelo paterno Agustin Carmona. (We get together for Christmas, the New Year and each family birthday. We've also adopted U.S. holidays, Thanksgiving, 4th of July, Easter and Holy Week, Valentine's Day and St. Patrick's Day. When my siblings and I were growing up we addressed our elders with the word *usted* (formal address) rather than the word *tu* (informal address) as they do now. Also, when we greeted our grandparents, parents and godparents we were obligated to kiss their hands as a sign of respect. It used to be customary that the eldest son was given the name of the father or grandfather; for example, my brother Agustin was named for our paternal grandfather, Agustin Carmona.

What We Love About Santa Fe

Bueno como e mencionado en mi diario, el llegar a una ciudad desconocida que me abrio sus brazos y su corazon, de la cual yo solo llega sabiento su nombre (santa fé) y despues ella es mi casa, mi hogar y el hogar de mis hermanos y mis hijos. Pienso que es una ciudad linda. (My arrival in this unknown city that opened its arms and heart to us in accordance with its name—City of the Holy Faith. Since then, this is the house and home of me, my siblings, and my children. It is a lovely city.)

Changes We'd Like to See

We'd like to see more houses and more affordable houses to accommodate new families. We'd like to see the different races and cultures respect each other more.

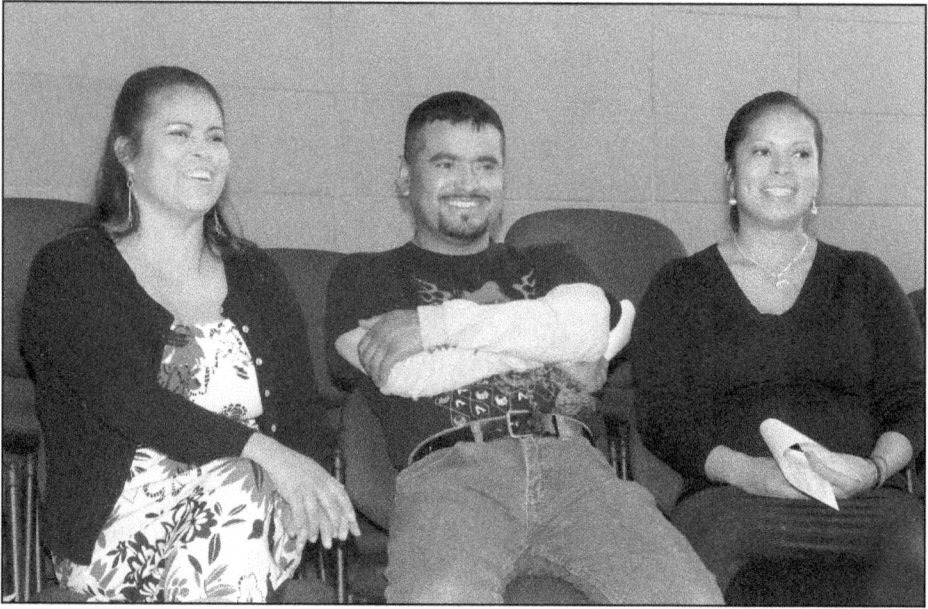

María, brother Agustin and daughter Marisela, 2008.

The Grass is Greener on the Other Side
by Heriberto Carmona

As a teen single mother I left my country
looking for a better life,
not knowing the hard times
I would have to endure
to get my dream.

I traveled from Zacatecas to Juaréz
to the U.S. Mexico border.
Rolling under the bridge,
avoiding the Las Migras spotlight,
I was groped by my best friend's boyfriend
who wouldn't leave me alone.
We jumped on a train
and lay down, bruising our legs.

Three times, crossing the river,
crossing over, I nearly got caught
or drowned. I didn't give up.

The grass is greener on the other side.

Arriving to a beautiful city named Santa Fe
I met a sweet old lady, Agnes Trujillo,
who offered me work and a home.

She fed me and found me work,
and I got on my feet.

The grass is greener on the other side.

I've built my life in this country.
I came when I was 21 and now I'm 41.
I am now a U.S. citizen with three kids
and three grandchildren
and my life changed for the better.

The grass IS greener on the other side.

La Hierba es Más Verde en el Otro Lado

Cuando yo estaba una madre joven sola
yo dejé mi país para la busca
una mejor vida, no sabiendo
los tiempos duros
que tendría que durar
conseguir mi sueño.

Yo viajé de Zacatecas a Juaréz y a la frontera.
Arrollando bajo el puente,

evitando el proyector de Las Migras,
yo fui tanteado por el novio
de mi mejor amiga
que no me dejaría en paz.
Saltamos en un tren y posamos,
magullándose nuestras piernas.

Tres veces, cruzando el río,
atravasando, yo casi fui agarrada
o ahogada. No me rendí.

La hierba es más verde en el otro lado.

Llegada a una ciudad hermosa llamó Santa Fe.
Encontré a una vieja señora dulce, Agnes Trujillo,
quien me ofreció el trabajo y un hogar.

Ella me alimentó, ella me encontró trabajo,
y subí a mis pies.

La hierba es más verde en el otro lado.

He construido mi vida en este país.
Vine cuando yo tenía 21 años y ahora tengo 41.
Ahora soy un ciudadana de los Estados Unidos
con tres niños y tres nietos
y mi vida cambió para bien.

La hierba es realmente más verde en el otro lado.

(Translation by Valerie and Exilda Martínez)

THE CARMONA FAMILY

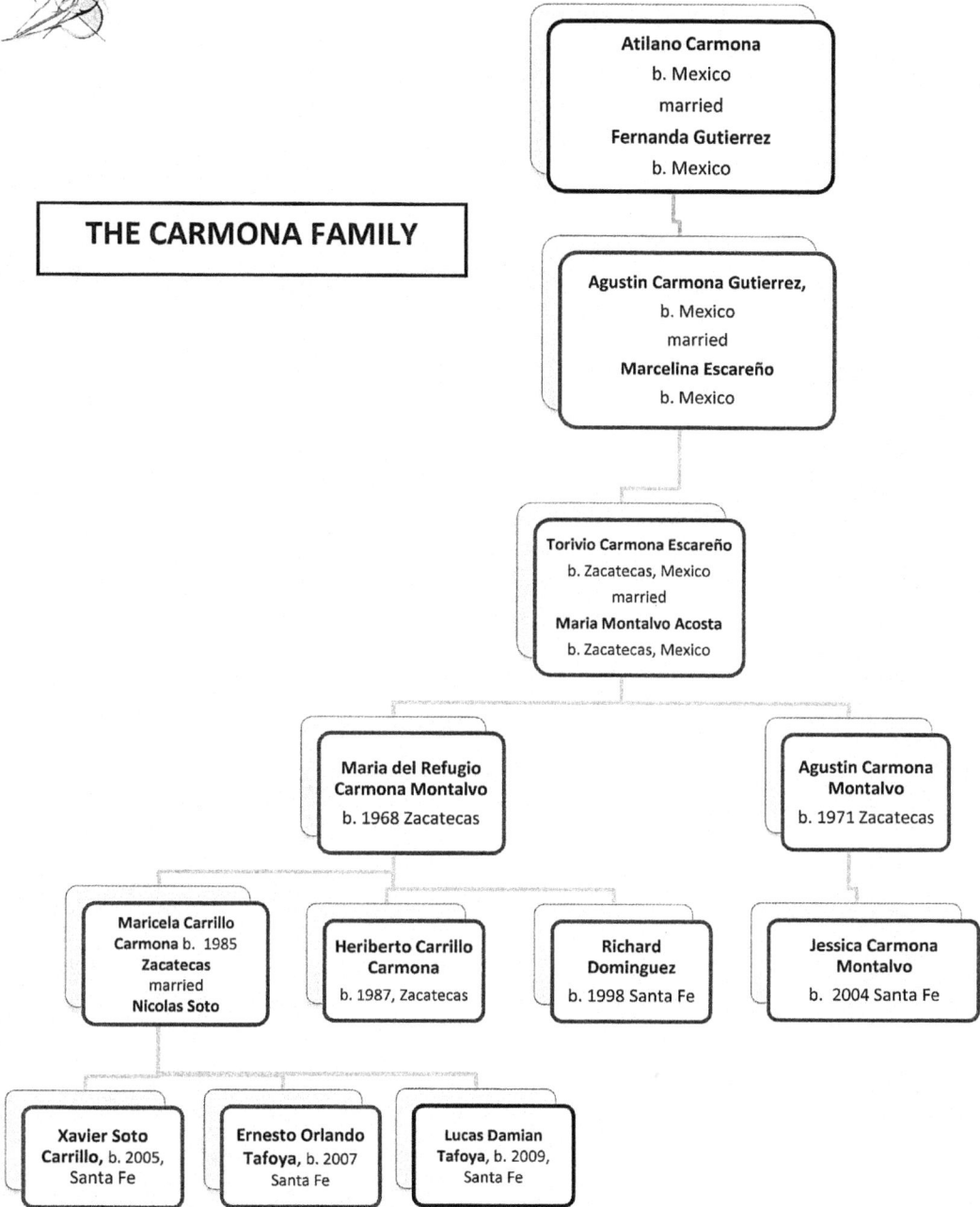

Atilano Carmona
b. Mexico
married
Fernanda Gutierrez
b. Mexico

Agustin Carmona Gutierrez,
b. Mexico
married
Marcelina Escareño
b. Mexico

Torivio Carmona Escareño
b. Zacatecas, Mexico
married
Maria Montalvo Acosta
b. Zacatecas, Mexico

Maria del Refugio Carmona Montalvo
b. 1968 Zacatecas

Agustin Carmona Montalvo
b. 1971 Zacatecas

Maricela Carrillo Carmona b. 1985 **Zacatecas** married **Nicolas Soto**

Heriberto Carrillo Carmona
b. 1987, Zacatecas

Richard Dominguez
b. 1998 Santa Fe

Jessica Carmona Montalvo
b. 2004 Santa Fe

Xavier Soto Carrillo, b. 2005, Santa Fe

Ernesto Orlando Tafoya, b. 2007 Santa Fe

Lucas Damian Tafoya, b. 2009, Santa Fe

The Goler Baca Family

Wedding of Fidel García and Flora Martínez, Santa Fe, 1926,
on the corner of Acequia Madre and Paseo de Peralta.

The Goler Baca Family

Participating Family Members and Ages

First Generation—Ana María Marcomini de Goler (*in memoriam*)

Second Generation—María de la Paz Goler Baca (47, married to Lawrence Baca de García)

Third Generation—Ellen Jane Baca (17)

Brief Family History
by
María Goler Baca

The Marcomini family (my maternal ancestors) came from Trencheto and Rovigo, Italy. They migrated to Buenos Aires, Argentina, where they completed their family of eleven. Most family members were merchants. Roberto Bruno Marcomini (my grandfather) worked for the circus. He was a ventriloquist, one-man-band, and clown.

The Goler family (my paternal ancestors) originated from Spain and the French Basque region and also migrated to Buenos Aires. They were bankers, artists and antique dealers. My father restored and sold antiques. Unhappy with the political situation, he wanted to get the family out of Buenos Aires and Argentina. He came to the United States in 1970 in search for a place for the family to live. Because of their art communities, he narrowed his choices to Atlanta and Santa Fe.

I remember the drive from Albuquerque when my brother, Victor, me and my mother first arrived in the United States. We kept repeating, "When are we going to get there?" Finally, my father (Gustavo) answered, "We are here." We looked around at the dirt roads and low-lying adobe houses. The beautiful blue skies and mountains were nowhere blocked by high-rise buildings. We were speechless; it looked nothing like what we expected.

The Baca and García families (my husband Lawrence's ancestors) go back to the time of the conquistadores. They came from Mexico and Spain. The families settled in Ojo de la Vaca, Moriarty, Galisteo, Lamy, Santa Rosa and, ultimately, Santa Fe. The García family (García St.) owned all the land from Acequia Madre to Canyon Road and Camino del Monte Sol. They raised sheep. The Baca family settled on Urioste Street. They raised sheep, cattle and horses and worked for the railroad.

Our families suffered tremendously when we lost Rosina Baca on Christmas Eve, 2005, and Ana Goler on the Epiphany, January 6, 2007. Their passing has forever changed the meaning of the Twelve Days of Christmas, and they have also made us reflect on the importance of our mothers and what they leave behind. This has inspired the piece we have created for the Lines and Circles project.

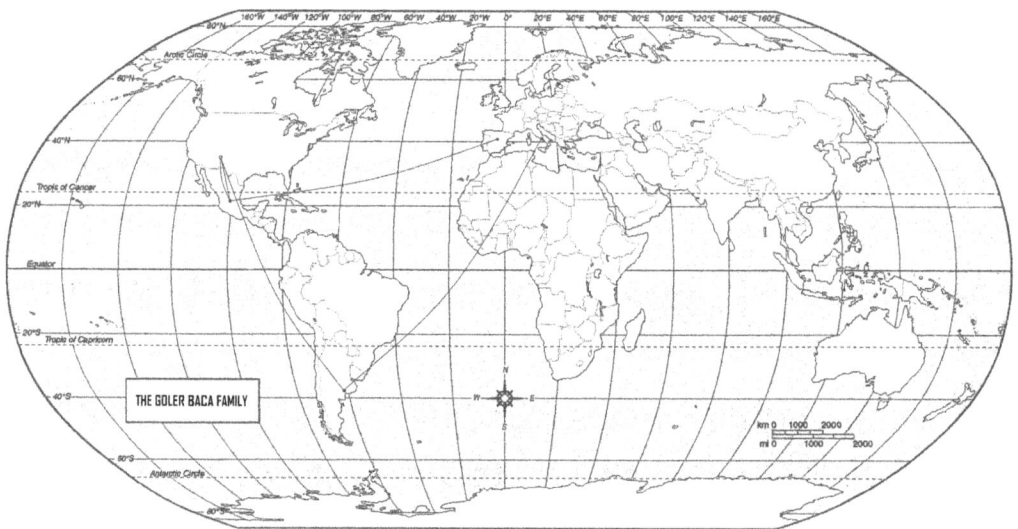

Family Heirlooms

Photographs, letters, mates (for drinking yerba mate) and bombillas (straw to drain and drink the tea), and jewelry.

Family Recipes

Chile caribe (Rosina), caldito and green chile stew (Paul), marinara sauce (Amalia), and milanesas (Ana).

What We Love About Santa Fe

The light and the beautiful architecture. The wildflowers, the mountains, and the Rio Grande. We love the history and our ancestors who passed down the traditions that make this town so special.

Changes We'd Like to See

We would like to see more of a sense of community and partnership with people who move to Santa Fe. We want them to respect the heritage and traditions that are the foundation of our historic and magical town.

The Goler Baca family in 2005

Mama Mia!
Si Senor!
by
Ellen Jane Baca

Life sends us through history
But our history is our life.
Families' roots grow and grow,
Traveling, living, and being.

Follow our branches to the heart of our tree,
You will dig up the Montes Vascos, Morenas
And Appenninos.

Marriage to marriage you will find yourself climbing
The Cordillera de los Andes and reaching the peaks
Of the the Sierra Madres.

Sliding down the cold flame mountainside,
Tierra del Fuego,
Splashing into Iguazu Falls
and rafting down
The Rio Grande.

To gloriously end this dig,
Climb the branches back up to the tips
And find yourself watching a sunset
Setting the mountains ablaze,
Sangre de Cristo,
In the thriving Plaza of Santa Fe.

Aqui llegamos!
Aqui estamos!

MARCOMINI-GOLER-BACA FAMILY

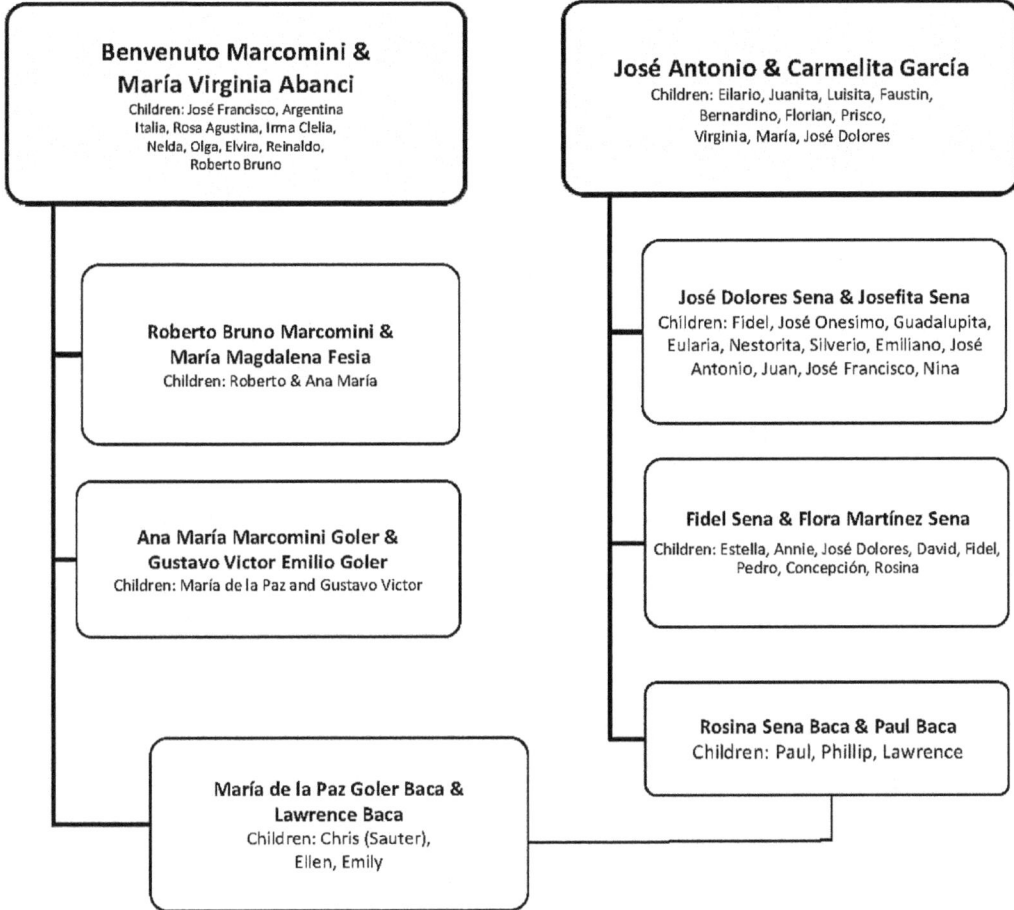

**Benvenuto Marcomini &
María Virginia Abanci**
Children: José Francisco, Argentina
Italia, Rosa Agustina, Irma Clelia,
Nelda, Olga, Elvira, Reinaldo,
Roberto Bruno

José Antonio & Carmelita García
Children: Eilario, Juanita, Luisita, Faustin,
Bernardino, Florian, Prisco,
Virginia, María, José Dolores

**Roberto Bruno Marcomini &
María Magdalena Fesia**
Children: Roberto & Ana María

José Dolores Sena & Josefita Sena
Children: Fidel, José Onesimo, Guadalupita,
Eularia, Nestorita, Silverio, Emiliano, José
Antonio, Juan, José Francisco, Nina

**Ana María Marcomini Goler &
Gustavo Victor Emilio Goler**
Children: María de la Paz and Gustavo Victor

Fidel Sena & Flora Martínez Sena
Children: Estella, Annie, José Dolores, David, Fidel,
Pedro, Concepción, Rosina

Rosina Sena Baca & Paul Baca
Children: Paul, Phillip, Lawrence

**María de la Paz Goler Baca &
Lawrence Baca**
Children: Chris (Sauter),
Ellen, Emily

The Gottlieb Shapiro Bachman Family

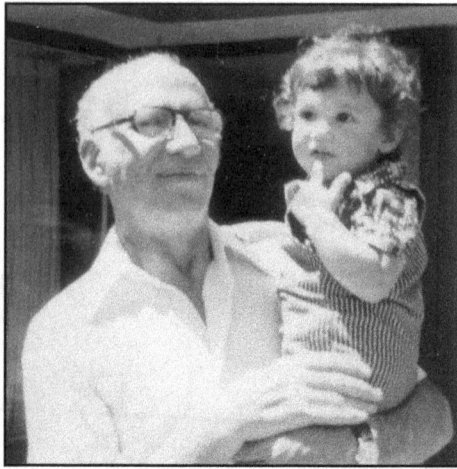

Grandpa "Papa" Meyer with Andrew, 1973.

The Gottlieb Shapiro Bachman Family

Participating Family Members and Ages

First Generation—Patricia Gottlieb Shapiro (65)
Second Generation—Margo Shapiro Bachman (35)
Third Generation—Sierra Gabriella Bachman (4)

Brief Family History
by Patricia Gottlieb Shapiro

Pat, Margo, and Sierra are descended from Boris and Anna Gottlieb, Pat's paternal grandparents. Boris and Anna Gottlieb had six children—Simon, David, Harry, Meyer, Eva and Celia. They lived in the small village of Miroslav, Lithuania, then under the rule of the Russian czar. Their simple home had no running water or electricity but had parquet floors and they had two maids to help with milking cows and housework. Boris dealt in grain and mortgages.

Sons Simon and David, both educated, went to Russia in their late teens and became active in the Communist party. Harry could not get into the United States so he traveled to Mexico and entered the U.S. through El Paso, where he stayed and raised his family. Boris and Anna and their two daughters were killed by the Nazis in World War II.

Pat's father, Meyer Gottlieb, left Lithuania at age 24, seeing no future for himself there. At that time, it was very hard for Jews to get an education or to succeed in business. He sailed to America, arriving in New York harbor on the evening of October 9, 1924. Seeing the Statue of Liberty and the city of New York in lights "was the most beautiful sight," he said. "I will never forget it as long as I live." After arriving on Ellis Island, he took a train to Chicago where his Uncle Simon met him and took him to Kenosha, Wisconsin where he had his first steak dinner. He learned English at night and drove a furniture truck by day for the company his uncle owned in Racine.

Meyer met his wife, Marge, while horseback riding. They married on December 27, 1942 in Harrisburg, PA where Meyer was stationed in the army at Indian Town Gap. When he was discharged the following year, they moved back to Racine. He worked his way up the company to become Vice President. His wife devoted herself to their family and did volunteer work.

Pat was born in 1944 and sister Anne in 1948. They shared a bedroom and at night when the lights were out; they loved to yak. Both good students, they went on to college and moved out of Racine. Pat went to Philadelphia for graduate school where she met Dick; they married on Thanksgiving Day 1969. Pat and Dick had children Andrew (1972) and Margo (1974). Raising their family was busy with baseball practice, gymnastics lessons, summer camp and family camping trips to New England. Andrew went to culinary school and settled in Long Island, where he lives with his wife Corrie and their two children. Margo, after college and world travel, ended up in Santa Fe where she met and married Nicolai Bachman. Their daughter Sierra will turn four in 2010. Two years after Margo moved to Santa Fe, Pat and Dick followed.

Today, Pat is a writer and yoga teacher and Dick is a retired psychotherapist. Margo is an Ayurvedic practitioner; husband Nicolai is a Sanskrit and yoga philosophy teacher. The Gottlieb Shapiro Bachman family continues their family traditions of connectedness, sharing and celebration.

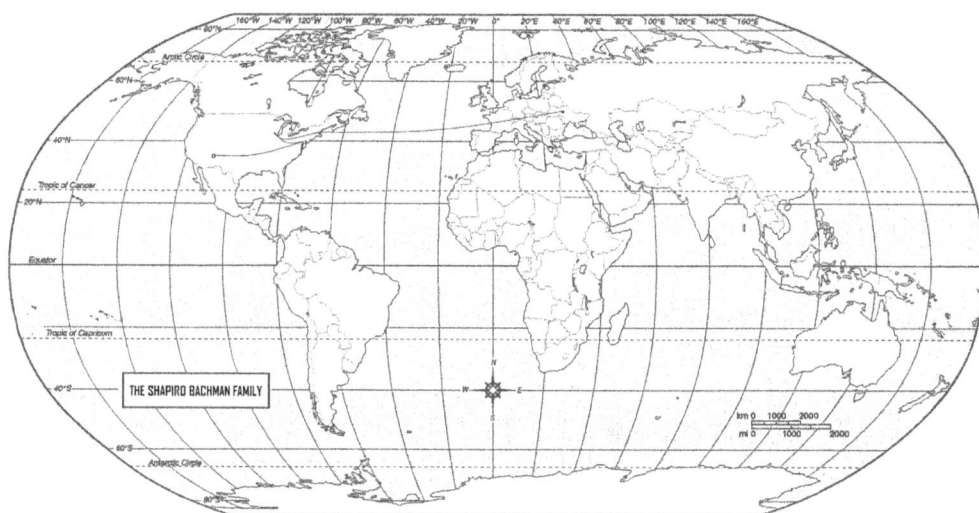

THE SHAPIRO BACHMAN FAMILY

Family Traditions

elebrating the Jewish holidays, marrying Jewish partners, going to the Jersey shore in the summer. We get together for Jewish holidays, birthdays, Thanksgiving and at other times. We eat, drink, and hang out. We try to take a family vacation every year or two or have a family reunion to include Margo's brother and his family who live in New York.

Family Heirlooms
Photos, furniture, Bible, menorahs, jewelry, and paintings.

Family Recipes
Matzo balls, potato pancakes (latkes), challah, lentil soup, bunny pancakes, cookie and whipped cream dessert.

What We Love About Santa Fe
Sunshine, blue skies, mountains, fresh clean air, culture, friendly people, and diversity.

What Troubles us About Our Hometown
The lack of water, development, the real estate market, and inconsistent schools.

The Shapiro Bachman Family Today

Searching for Family
by
Pat Shapiro

I'm your first cousin, she wrote,
Simon's daughter from Russia.
Who knew we had family
alive after the war?

Simon's daughter from Russia
told of four brothers separated.
We had family alive after the war
Simon and David to Russia,
imprisoned and shot.

She told of four brothers separated.
Harry and Meyer thrived in America
Simon and David to Russia,
imprisoned and shot.
Widow Tatjana, 93, still strong.

Harry and Meyer thrived in America
now, four brothers dead,
widow Tatjana, 93, still strong,
and a survivor searching for family.

Now, four brothers dead.
I'm your first cousin, she wrote,
a survivor searching for family.
Who knew?

THE SHAPIRO BACHMAN FAMILY

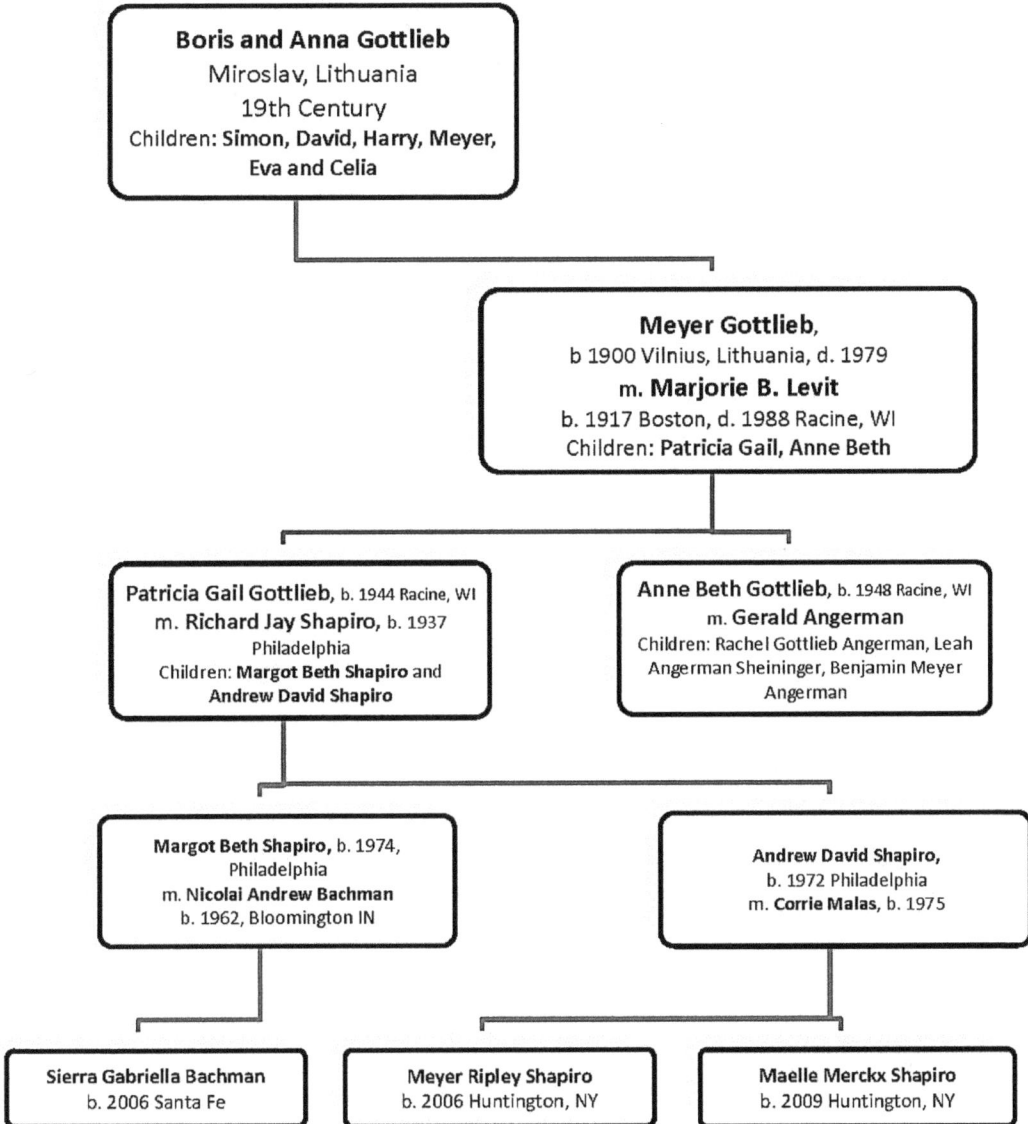

Boris and Anna Gottlieb
Miroslav, Lithuania
19th Century
Children: **Simon, David, Harry, Meyer,
Eva and Celia**

Meyer Gottlieb,
b 1900 Vilnius, Lithuania, d. 1979
m. **Marjorie B. Levit**
b. 1917 Boston, d. 1988 Racine, WI
Children: **Patricia Gail, Anne Beth**

Patricia Gail Gottlieb, b. 1944 Racine, WI
m. **Richard Jay Shapiro**, b. 1937
Philadelphia
Children: **Margot Beth Shapiro** and
Andrew David Shapiro

Anne Beth Gottlieb, b. 1948 Racine, WI
m. **Gerald Angerman**
Children: Rachel Gottlieb Angerman, Leah
Angerman Sheininger, Benjamin Meyer
Angerman

Margot Beth Shapiro, b. 1974,
Philadelphia
m. **Nicolai Andrew Bachman**
b. 1962, Bloomington IN

Andrew David Shapiro,
b. 1972 Philadelphia
m. **Corrie Malas**, b. 1975

Sierra Gabriella Bachman
b. 2006 Santa Fe

Meyer Ripley Shapiro
b. 2006 Huntington, NY

Maelle Merckx Shapiro
b. 2009 Huntington, NY

The Ingram Family

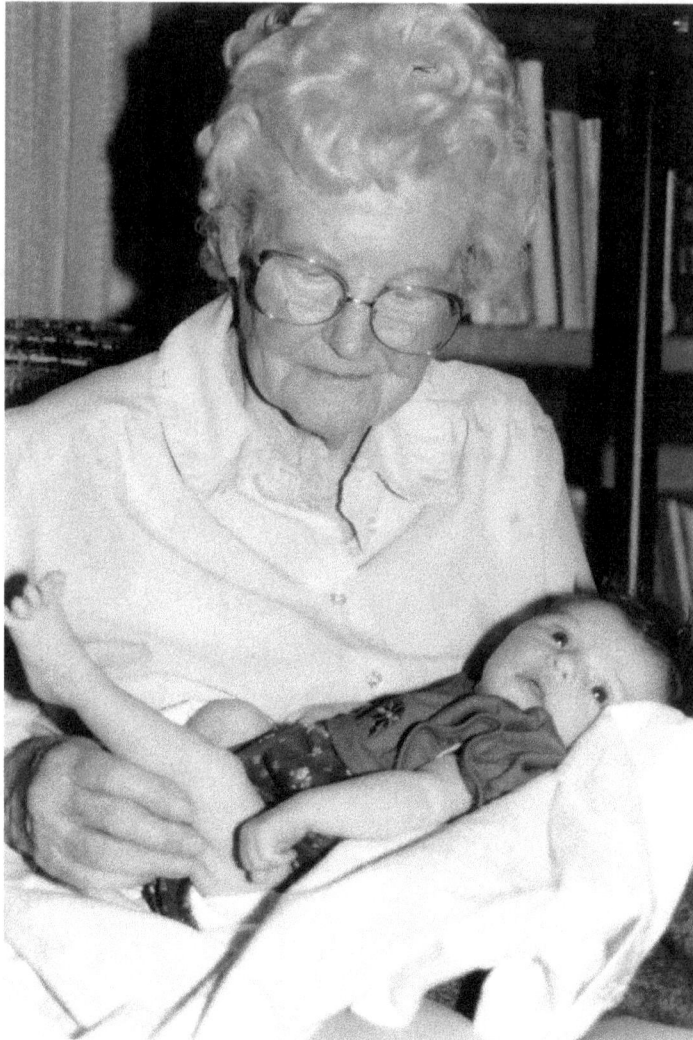

Hazel Ingram with great-granddaughter Amanda, 1998

The Ingram Family

Participating Family Members and Ages

First Generation—Barbara Ingram (65)
Second Generation—Valerie Ingram (42), Carolyn Ingram (40), Heather Ingram (38)
Third Generation—Rick (9) and Joshua (6) Pringle (sons of Valerie), Amanda (11) and Alexander (3) Jacobs (children of Carolyn), Donnie Slack (3) and Barbara Isabelle (3 months) Slack (children of Heather)

Brief Family History
by
Hazel Elizabeth Reynolds Ingram in 1986

"*M*y mother married my father when she lacked one month of being fifteen and he was twenty-six. In the twelve or thirteen years they were married before my father died, there were five of us born. My father had gone from Gatebo, Oklahoma to Burkburnett, Texas to work in the oil fields. This was at the end of the first World War when every community was plagued by the terrible flu which the soldiers brought from Europe. My father died in 1919 of this flu.

We received a telegram for my mother to go. Of course, we had no money and since the creeks and rivers were flooding my father's brother could not cross to our house. My uncle had a telephone and he had received the message. I can remember all of us standing on our side and Uncle Ray on the other shouting across. My mother had no decent shoes and Uncle Ray threw a pair of Aunt Frances' across and threw some money in a bag weighted with rocks. My mother went by train and when they got to Red River all passengers had to walk across on the railroad ties because the flood had damaged the bridge. The train made it across very slowly.

In a few days my father died. He was buried in Duncan, Oklahoma. I remember standing by the grave, but I didn't understand what it was all about. The worst part was when we went back to Uncle Ray's house across the creek. Mama went upstairs and she just cried her heart out. Oh, I can still hear her sobs.

We moved to Elida, New Mexico where my Grandfather Coleman had a ranch. Not long after we moved to New Mexico my grandfather died and the ranch was sold. We, along with my grandmother, moved to Portales. My mother washed, ironed and cleaned house for several different families. Most of the time my mother could manage meat on Sunday but other days we ate beans, potatoes, macaroni with tomatoes, cornbread, biscuits, gravy (made with canned milk) and whatever vegetables my mother could grow in her garden. We had chickens and she canned and dried fruit for the winter months.

After a couple of years in Portales, we moved to Albuquerque where my mother worked in a cafeteria. There were no laws on the hours a person could work, so it was not unusual for those women to work twelve or fourteen hours. I've never been able to figure out how she was able to finish a secretarial course at business school. While the Legislature was in session she was secretary to Mr. Praegar, a State Senator.

We moved to Roswell from Albuquerque. My mother opened a small café in Roswell which was the first time I saw the man who I eventually married. He was delivering milk products for Clardy's Dairy and delivered milk to our café. I was only fourteen, but he told someone that I was the one he would marry. So he waited almost a year before he asked me for a date. Then when he came I was off somewhere with a bunch of kids. Poor mama was so embarrassed. He didn't try again for almost a year. Can you blame him? I can't even imagine why he bothered with me at all since I was so silly. We dated for several months over a year before I would let him kiss me. You can't believe that in this day, probably. We were married on August 15, 1930 when I was seventeen and had graduated from high school.

I may have been a silly girl but I believe I made a good wife and mother and a good housekeeper. Anyway I never heard differently from anyone."

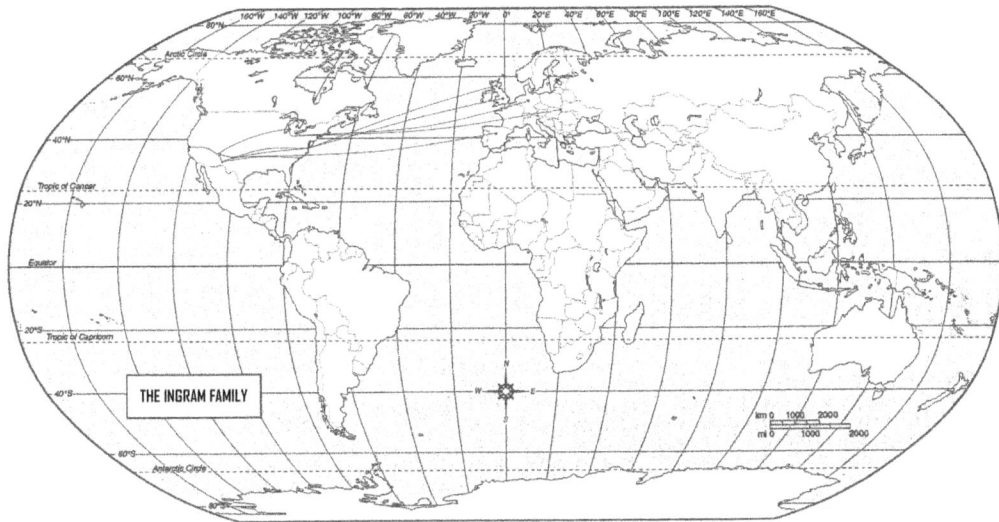

THE INGRAM FAMILY

Family Traditions

Summer vacations at the family cabin in Taos County; homemade ice cream; opening one present (just one!) on Christmas Eve; political discussions at the dinner table; gatherings at Heather Ingram and Don Slack's home in Albuquerque for the Fourth of July for swimming, fajitas, and fireworks; holiday gatherings with much advance planning around who will cook what dish; we have sometimes used family names to honor our ancestors.

Family Heirlooms
From Valerie down to Donnie, all the family infants have slept in the same cradle.

Family Recipes
Grammy's Chocolate Cake and Grammy's Taco Soup.

What We Love About Santa Fe
Its sheer beauty, especially after we return home from traveling. The benefits of growing up in a multicultural community, again especially after visiting other areas of the country. We like the fact that Santa Fe is still a small city even though it's grown tremendously in three generations. Santa Feans are caring and everyone seems to have a cause they believe in.

What Troubles Us About Our Hometown

The rise of national and chain stores have forced locally-owned businesses to close. Population growth and the declining quality of public schools. Lack of health insurance for many. Problems stemming from poverty, including kids entering school poorly prepared. In Santa Fe, there is a growing divide between wealthy and poor families.

The Ingram Family 2009.

Who Will Tell Her
by
Valerie Ingram

Gold aspen leaves will be falling
              scattering
when she comes.

She won't know
what came before.

Who will tell her
of a milk delivery man
and the twelve-year-old girl at her mother's café?

Who will tell her
of the girl's plea to her mother
at the age of 14 to marry that man?

Who will tell her
of six children
red hair
wrapping butter, five cents a case?

Who will tell her
of the red brick house on Fourth Street?
        merry-go-round and swimming in the stock tank
        closet full of comic books

Who will tell her
of the eldest who sought a career in DC
and instead brought home a wife?
        spent all night talking
        watched the sun rise behind
        the Washington monument

Who will tell her
how the wife dusted a tiny apartment
        every day
wondering when the New Mexico wind
would stop?

Who will tell her
how dinners around a long wooden table
shaped our opinions?

The leaves fall another season
        and I worry no one will remember
        who came before.

Who will tell her
where she comes from?

I will.

You will.

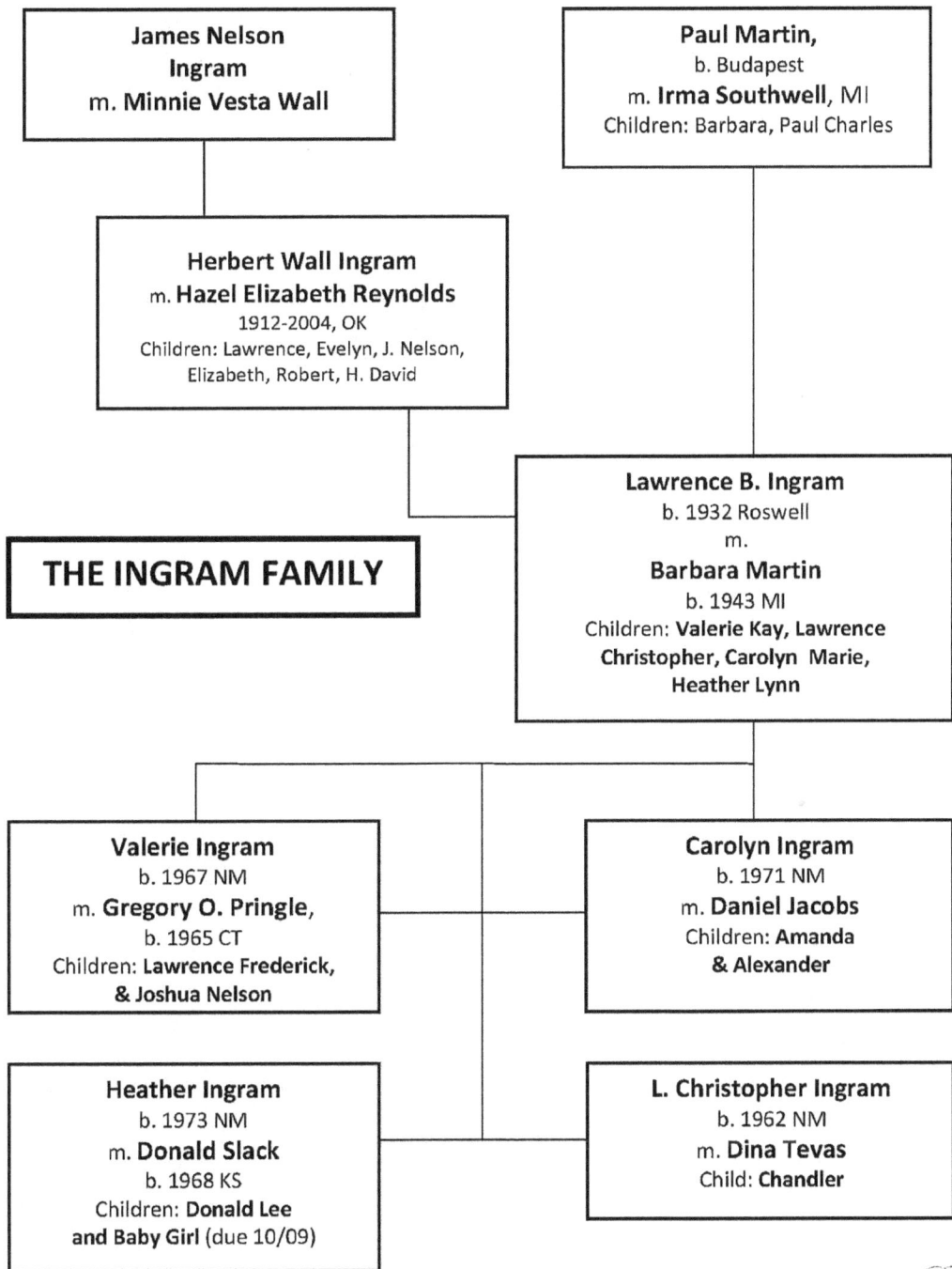

James Nelson
Ingram
m. **Minnie Vesta Wall**

Paul Martin,
b. Budapest
m. **Irma Southwell**, MI
Children: Barbara, Paul Charles

Herbert Wall Ingram
m. **Hazel Elizabeth Reynolds**
1912-2004, OK
Children: Lawrence, Evelyn, J. Nelson,
Elizabeth, Robert, H. David

THE INGRAM FAMILY

Lawrence B. Ingram
b. 1932 Roswell
m.
Barbara Martin
b. 1943 MI
Children: **Valerie Kay, Lawrence
Christopher, Carolyn Marie,
Heather Lynn**

Valerie Ingram
b. 1967 NM
m. **Gregory O. Pringle**,
b. 1965 CT
Children: **Lawrence Frederick,
& Joshua Nelson**

Carolyn Ingram
b. 1971 NM
m. **Daniel Jacobs**
Children: **Amanda
& Alexander**

Heather Ingram
b. 1973 NM
m. **Donald Slack**
b. 1968 KS
Children: **Donald Lee
and Baby Girl** (due 10/09)

L. Christopher Ingram
b. 1962 NM
m. **Dina Tevas**
Child: **Chandler**

The Jones Brown Family

A man's home is his castle

Florenceruth and Mary Cay Jones, Fiesta de Santa Fe, 1943.

The Jones Brown Family

The Jones Brown Family

Participating Family Members and Ages

First Generation—Florenceruth "Flossie" Jones Brown (80)

Second Generation—William Harold Brown (54), John Howard Brown (52), Karen Schumm Brown (54), Ruth Brown Jimenez (50)

Third Generation—John Fredrick Pershing Brown (27), Tim Brendan Harris Brown (24), Gregory Ashton Whelan Brown (22)

Brief Family History
by Ruth Brown Jimenez)

Flossie's grandfather, William Jones, came from Ireland to Boston in the 1820's and was the primary contractor on the Illinois State Penitentiary in Joliet, Illinois. Flossie's father, Bill Jones (born in Joliet in 1898), received a seminary education and then worked for the Chicago Tribune. On a trip in 1929 through Santa Fe, he met Ruth Bush (also of Chicago) who had arrived in New Mexico in 1926 accompanying a friend who was ill with tuberculosis. Ms. Bush acted as New Mexico's Deputy State Bank Examiner in the 1920's and had a lifelong career with the U.S. Forest Service, creating the publicity campaign for Smokey the Bear. Bill and Ruth married in 1929 and had three children, Flossie, Bill, and Mary Cay. Bill got a job as a newspaper editor in Raton but the paper folded in two weeks. Flossie became very sick and the family drove her down to St. Vincent's Hospital in Santa Fe where she was diagnosed with pre-TB (which turned out, later, to be brucellosis caused by raw milk). In desperation, Bill Jones tried to sell insurance and Ruth got a job with a New Deal agency and worked at night at St. Vincent's to pay for Flossie's care. Flossie remembers that "Bill and Mary Cay were babysat in the St.Vincent Orphanage and Ruth Bush started a Girl Scout Troop there. I met Eleanor Roosevelt there when the Sisters of Charity and Mom were showing the First Lady the Orphanage."

Later, Flossie went to St. Francis School, Harrington Jr. High, and graduated from Loretto Academy in 1947. She attended UNM from 1948-1950, graduating with a B.A. in Economics. She entered UNM Law School and graduated 3rd in the class of 1953. She is currently the second longest admitted female attorney in New Mexico.

In 1954, Flossie married Herb Brown whose grandfather, William Herr Brown, was a descendant of the abolitionist John Brown. William Herr married Lillian Corinne Pershing, a niece of John "Blackjack" Pershing, General of the Armies during WWI. Flossie and Herb have three children, William, John and Ruth. John married Karen Schumm and they have three children, John, Tim, and Greg. Ruth married Christopher Jimenez, whose family originates in the Caribbean.

Members of the Brown and Church families live on land south of Santa Fe which was homesteaded in the 1920's by Bill Jones and Ruth Bush. In 1935 Bill Jones saw a government handout that announced that, under the Lincoln Homestead Act, all remaining lands except Nevada and Alaska would be withdrawn from settlement and revert to the public lands office. Bill moved quickly and registered their 120 acres, south of Santa Fe, with just days to go before the withdrawal. The family affectionately calls the property (now 140 acres) "Browncastle Ranch." Part of the property, today, comprises the Santa Fe Skies RV Park, owned and operated by the Brown family.

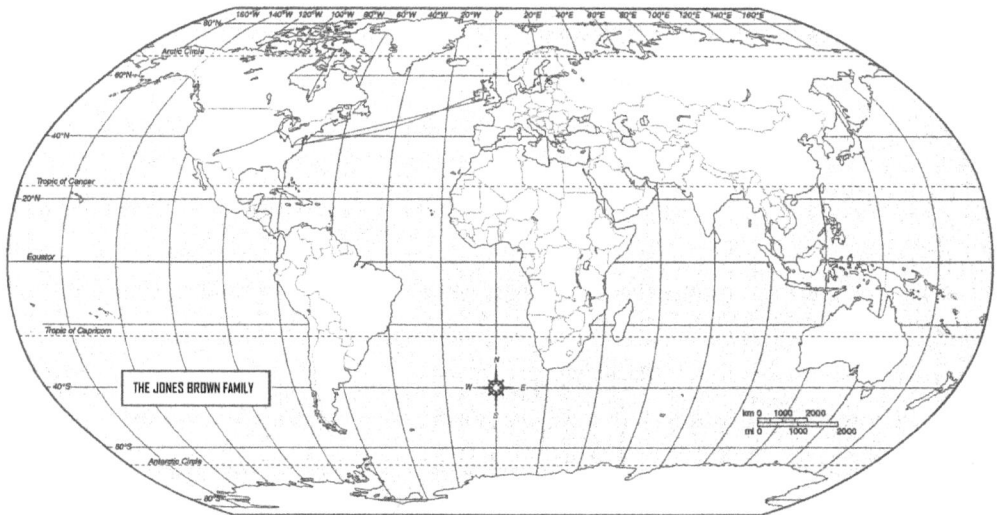

THE JONES BROWN FAMILY

Family Traditions

embers of the Jones Brown family build their own houses and fix their own cars; they wouldn't think of hiring anyone else to do so. Most family members are motorcyclists and compete in motorcycle contests. The family collects antique gas engines and each 4th of July Willie Brown and his fellow "Rusty Nuts" (members of the National Gas Engine Association) fire them up. The family is well known not only for on-the-road adventures (and frequent vehicle break-downs) but for coming to the rescue of family, friends, and acquaintances who call when they're stuck. "Go get the wrecker!" was a common phrase when Herb Brown was alive, and family members would walk or hitch back to Browncastle Ranch and drive the wrecker to those who needed help. Family travel, both nationally and internationally, is common. With their busy lives, the family does manage to get together for Thanksgiving. The most important family tradition, perhaps, is running the business of the Santa Fe Skies RV Park and life on the land at Browncastle Ranch.

Family Recipes

Oatmeal Raisin Cookies (for the girls in Flossie's Girl Scout Troops), Pumpkin Chiffon Pie, Cranberry Fluff Pie, Frito Pies.

What We Love About Santa Fe

The land, especially the wide open spaces so close to the city; Santa Fe's character; no big signs or billboards to ruin the look of the place; architectural "rules" that maintain the city's beauty; the friendly atmosphere; the lack of industry (big industry goes to Albuquerque); the Franciscan adobe style of Protestant churches; the relaxed and warm attitude toward illegal immigrants; beautiful sunsets every night, and the climate—it's never too hot or too cold; there's never too much or too little rain or snow; no tornadoes, hurricanes or other natural disasters; it's one of the safest zones in the world. Also, the Brown children grew up and went to school with kids of all backgrounds and ethnicities so friendships and conflicts were based on a person's character and not on race or class.

Changes We'd Like to See

More imagination on the part of the young people in Santa Fe. They say there's nothing to do and want to get away but the Brown children and grandchildren believe Santa Fe has most everything at its doorstep—roads to wander, dams and lakes to boat, mountains to hike, museums, art, and everything else.

The Jones Brown Family Today

A Man's Home is His Castle
by
Valerie Martínez

I take Highway 14 to Vista del Monte to Browncastle Road
then the ranch unfolds under the steady watch of the llano,
the Sangre de Cristos, the horizon circling for miles.

The Santa Fe Skies Park is bustling with RV's, friendly tourists,
seasonal regulars who tell me, knowingly, how to proceed
to Flossie Brown's house, one of seven homes in succession
to the north. I pass clusters of old engines like sculptures,
the Antique Gas Engine Display that Willie Brown hauls
to shows around the west. Land and sky open wide.

I sit at the table with Flossie and son John, descendants
on one side from abolitionist, Preacher John Brown,
and on the other from the Sharkey brothers who migrated
from Ireland in the 1860's. Mother and grandmother
was Ruth Bush Jones, the "Mother of Smokey Bear",
and Flossie, the second longest woman attorney
admitted in New Mexico, is a retired Assistant Attorney General.

Flossie drives me around Browncastle Ranch—homesteaded
in the 20's, saved in the nick of time from the '35 Lincoln
Homestead Act—and with such pride I understand, again,
the fierceness with which we root ourselves in a place
all our lives. John finds a photo of the ranch from the air,

and there I see the history of a family, land to home to business,
in a setting characterized by space between mountains,
the echo of a creek bed, the modern-day traffic of travelers
come to linger in a place where everything is earth and breath.

Weeks later I sit at the center of the Brown family chatter,
on the patio outside the RV park offices, great room, kitchen,
showers and bathrooms. Grandmother, sons and daughters,
grandsons, talk to and over each other, tease me, feed me
family trees, history, a sketch with helmet, gears, wrench,
shovel and a feather penning the phrases "to thine own self
be true" and "a man's house is his castle." Customers wander

in and out asking for change, mini-conversations start up,
another Santa Fe sunset highlights our skin and hair a shade
of pink, and if you ever want to feel the magnetic pull
of family, love of place, the tornado of family work
and business, take the road to Browncastle Ranch,
park your car, and call for someone with the last name
Brown. She will hold out a hand; he will tell you
what you need to know; they will regale you
with stories and make their castle your home.

Owen Brown
b. 1771 Connecticut
m. **Ruth Mills**, b. 1771

Sharkey Brothers, b. Ireland
migrated to PA then IL (Chicago)
in the 1860's

John Brown (Abolitionist) b. 1800 CT
m. **Dianthe Lusk** (died) then married
Mary Day Brown

Catherine Sharkey, b. late 1800's,
Ireland, migrated to U.S.,
married
Thomas Grant Bush, b. KY

Zachariah Brown, b 1822 PA
m. **Nancy M. Black**

Ruth Mary Bush Jones,
the mother of Smokey Bear,
b. 1903 Chicago
m. **William Michael Jones,**
b. 1898, IL
Children: **Florenceruth,** William,
Mary Catherine

William Herr Brown, b. 1852 OH
m. **Lillian Corinne Pershing**, b. 1857 IN

Florenceruth Jones, b. 1929 Chicago m.
Herbert Eugene Brown,
b. 1929 CO
Children: **William Harold,
Ruth Marie, John Howard**

Harold Edwin Brown, b. 1891 IN
m. **Marie Agnes Harris**, b. 1900 IN

John Howard Brown,
b. 1957 Santa Fe
m. **Karen Schumm**

Children: **John Fredrick Pershing, Timothy
Brendan Harris,
Gregory Ashton Whelan**

Herbert Eugene Brown, b. 1929 CO
m. **Florenceruth Jones Brown**
b. 1929 IL
Children: **Willam Harold, Ruth Marie,
John Howard**

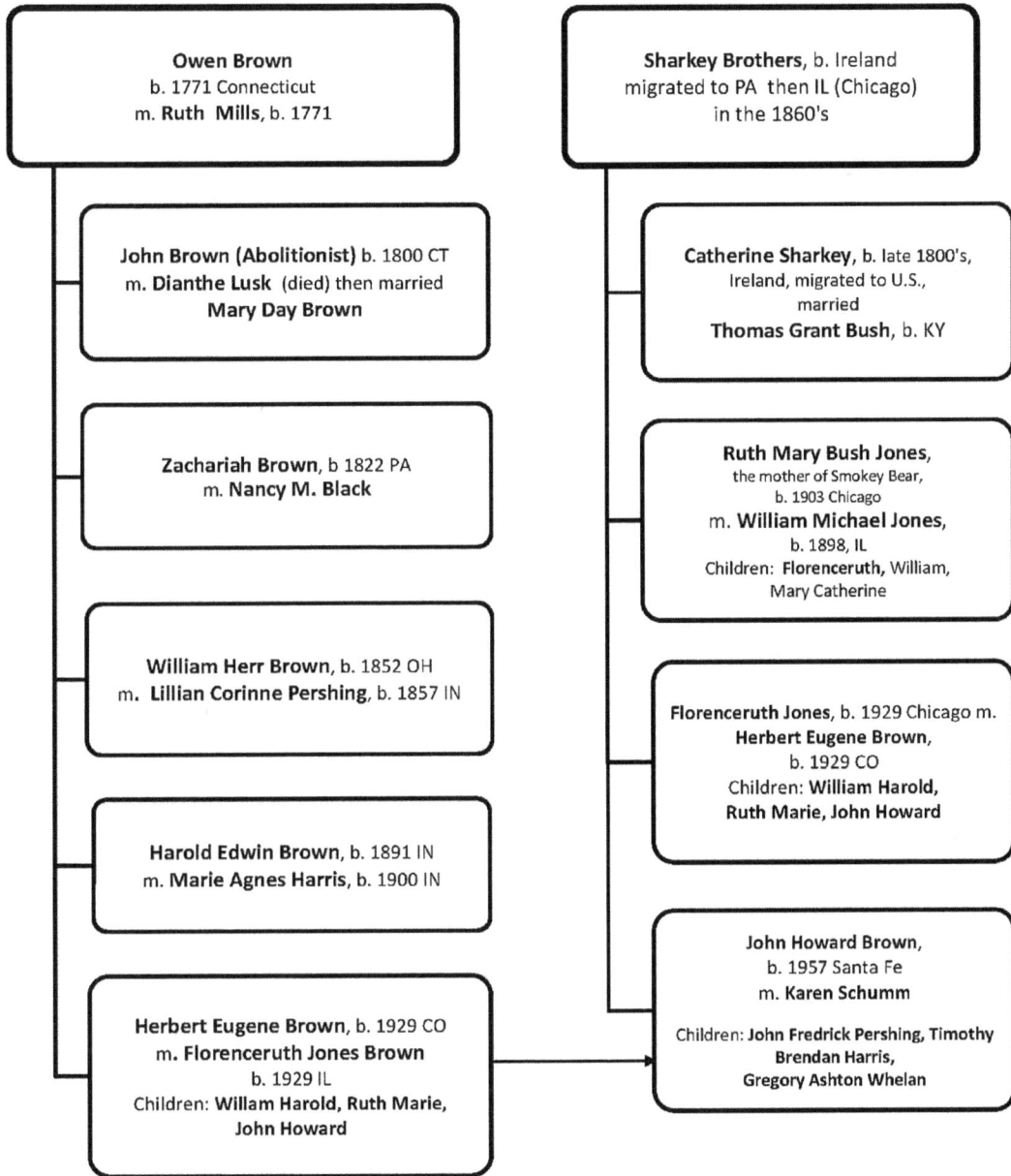

The Sharkey
Jones Brown Family

The Martinez Ridgley Family

*José María and Matiana Martínez on
their wedding day, Santa Fe, 1929.*

*Charles Herbert Ridgley and Margaret Sparling
Ridgley on their wedding day, Indiana, 1924.*

The Martínez Ridgley Family

Participating Family Members and Ages

First Generation—Agnes Alice Salazar Quintana de Trujillo (91)
Second Generation—Exilda Marie Trujillo Salazar de Martínez (70), José Ramón Martínez (77), Robert Ridgley (75), Marilyn Ridgley (74)
Third Generation—Andrea Martínez (*in memoriam*), Valerie Martínez (48), Jennifer Renée Martínez (46), José Ramón Martínez (46), James Martínez (45), John Martínez (43); Gregory Ridgley (47)
Fourth Generation—Niall Estevan Martínez Ridgley (13), Serafina Anne Martínez Ridgley (11)

Brief Family History
by
Exilda Martínez, Renée Martínez, and Gregory C. Ridgley

The Martínez and Salazar families have lived in northern New Mexico for thirteen generations. Our European ancestors came from Spain in the 1500's and early 1600's as part of the Spanish colonization of the "New World." Several Salazars traveled as soldiers with Don Juan de Oñate to San Juan, the first Spanish capital of New Mexico, in 1598. Our Martínez ancestors traveled from Spain to Zacatecas, Mexico, and later migrated north and settled in the late 1600s in New Mexico. Our ancestors were sheepherders, farmers, midwives, curanderas and, later, politicians, teachers, gamblers, and businessmen.

Today, Ramon and Exilda Martínez and three of their six children (Valerie, Renée and Ray) as well as five grandchildren live in or near Santa Fe. Ramon and Exilda devoted their adult lives to teaching in the Santa Fe Public Schools.

José Ramon Martínez was born in 1932, the second of eight children born to José María Martínez and Matiana Martínez. He was a gifted student and athlete and attended St. Michael's High School, St. Michael's College, and New Mexico Highlands University. Ramon's father, José Maria Martínez owned the Martínez Supermarket on Agua Fria Street from 1956 to 1970.

Exilda Marie Trujillo y Salazar was born in 1939, the precocious first child of Agnes Salazar and Ismael Trujillo. Her maternal grandparents, Don Diego y Doña Serafina Salazar were a big influence in her life. Don Diego was mayor of Española from 1936 to 1950. Doña Serafina played the organ and led the choir at the Sacred Heart Church. Exilda attended Loretto Academy, College of Santa Fe, and the University of New Mexico.

The Ridgley and Hester branches of the family are of northern European origin. Ridgley ancestors came to North America from the 17th through 19th centuries from the British Isles and Germany. Hester ancestors arrived from Ireland in the mid-19th century. Over the last hundred years, family members have lived in the Midwest, New England, upstate New York, California, the Pacific Northwest, and New Mexico.

James Weston Ridgley (1802-1866) and his wife Christina Brandenburg Ridgley (1801-1877) moved from Montgomery County, Ohio and homesteaded the Ridgley family farm in Wabash County, Indiana in 1841. Four generations of the family lived on this farm, including Charles Herbert Ridgley, Greg's grandfather.

Michael Augustus Hester, Sr. came to the United States in 1864 from Louisburg, County Mayo, Ireland. Michael and Bridget Keane Hester raised eight children, including Joseph Paul Hester, on a 30-acre farm near Groton, in upstate New York.

Members of the Ridgley and Hester families came to Santa Fe after Gregory Ridgley married Renée Martínez and the couple moved to New Mexico in 1992. Greg's parents, Robert Louis Ridgley and Marilyn Hester Ridgley, came to Santa Fe soon thereafter. Bob was born in Fort Wayne, Indiana to Charles Herbert and Margaret Sparling Ridgley. He met Marilyn at high school in Binghamton, New York. Marilyn's mother, Mary Walpole Hester, was a teacher, and her father, Joseph Paul Hester, worked as an attorney and executive for the Endicott-Johnson Shoe Company. Bob and Marilyn were married in 1957.

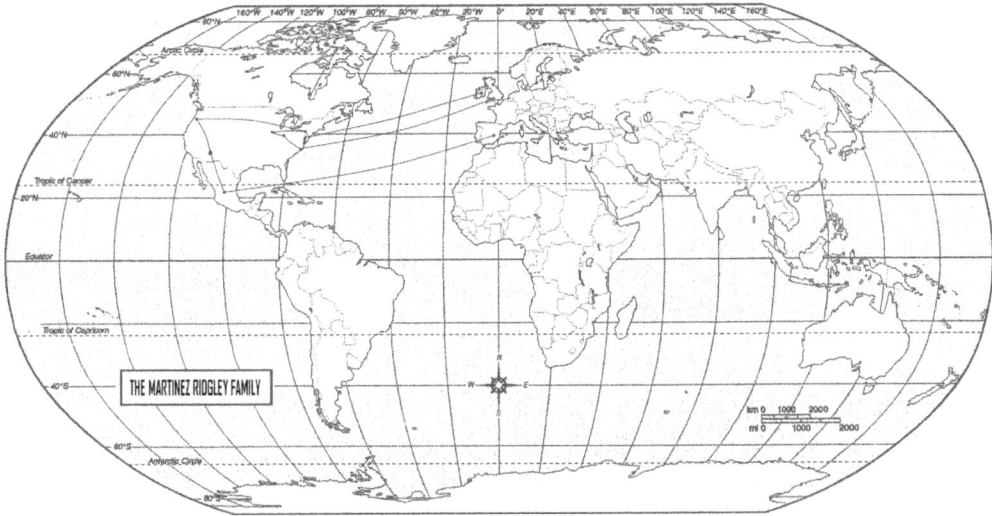

THE MARTINEZ RIDGLEY FAMILY

Family Traditions

artínez: Baptisms (and the tradition of godparents); First Holy Communions; family reunions (on the Martínez and Salazar sides of the family); attending and/or participating in the Santa Fe Fiesta; Agnes and Exilda are members of La Sociedad Folklorica and the family usually attends its Baile de Cascaronas; family gatherings at Easter, Thanksgiving and especially Christmas, when tamale-making involves a production line of great grandmas, grandmas, mothers, daughters, granddaughters and, occasionally, brave sons-in-laws and grandsons. The baking of special desserts including empanaditas, biscochitos and pastelitos. Our traditional Christmas Eve family meal is posole with red chile and tortillas; on Christmas Day it is ham, turkey, mashed potatoes, jello salad, pumpkin and pecan pies. We exchange presents on Christmas Eve and the kids wake up on Christmas Day to open gifts from Santa Claus. For many years, the family held a tradition of attending a special Christmas Eve midnight mass at the downtown Cathedral Basilica of St. Francis of Assisi. Jose Ramón remembers walking home as a child, after midnight mass and having empanaditas and coffee when he arrived, even the kids! *Ridgley*: Saturday morning pancakes; getting together for Thanksgiving or Christmas holidays; father-son trips to see Boston Red Sox games; intergenerational vacation travel.

Family Heirlooms

Martínez: Silver coffee pots, punchbowls and serving sets; antique rings and watches; Navajo rugs; Exilda's wedding dress.

Ridgley: George Washington Ridgley's letters home to his wife Catherine during his service in the Civil War; James Weston Ridgley's saddlebags; an 1875 Wabash County Atlas; Ridgley family Bible; C.H. Ridgley's boyhood hunting rifle; Orrin Ridgley's watch; Sparling and Ridgley family furniture; Joe Hester's traveling trunk; Nora Ridgley's trousseau trunk; Anna Walpole's Toy Doll Chest and sewing machine; Anna Walpole's paintings; Margaret Sparling Ridgley's paintings and hooked rug; Anna Walpole's bedroom set; Margaret Sparling Ridgley's silver spoon collection from all over the world, and a wire toy figurine made by Marilyn Hester for her uncle Donald Walpole and carried by Donald on all his WWII bombing runs.

Family Recipes

Martínez: Biscochitos, Tortillas, Sopapillas, Empanaditas (with cow's tongue mincemeat or fruit filling), Pastelitos, Natillas, Posole, Calabacitas. Agnes and Exilda made/make the most delicious red chile sauce and tamales that melt in your mouth.

Ridgley: Marilyn Ridgley's German Pancakes and Anna Walpole's Irish Soda Bread.

What We Love About Santa Fe

Martínez: Its natural beauty—the mountains, high-desert climate, blue sky, the changing of color of aspen leaves in the fall, afternoon thunderstorms in the summer, snow. We love its fascinating history including the indigenous peoples and cultures, first Spanish colonization, Pueblo Revolt, Spanish Reconquest, change of governments (Spain, France, Mexico, United States), and transition from small town to art mecca. We love the fact that Spanish is spoken both by newer (Mexican) immigrants and older families. We love Santa Fe's arts (opera, music, museums, galleries) and entertainment (e.g. film), the appeal of a big city in a small city.

Ridgley: Four hundred years of history unique in North America; the mountains; Santa Fe is still a small town in many ways, but with cultural institutions and amenities usually only found in much larger cities; easy access to the outdoors; mild southern Rockies climate; cultural diversity and tolerance; good food.

What Troubles Us about Our Hometown

Martínez: There are fewer gathering places and events where families from all backgrounds mingle and work together. There is tension, sometimes, between immigrant and older Hispanic families. The high cost of living makes it difficult for lower income families to live in Santa Fe.

Ridgley: Lack of outrage over troubled public schools; how little Santa Fe's diverse ethnic and cultural communities really interact.

Gregory Ridgley and Renee Martínez on their wedding day, Tesuque, 1990.

Letters to Wherever You Are
by Valerie Martínez

We write: *Dear Kate, Dear Grandma,*
Dear Diego, Dear Sister Andrea,

as if paper and ink travel the air
between now and then, here
and wherever you are.

What we did not say, couldn't,
wished we'd said, now have to—

I want you to know, remember,
it's clear now, everything you said

flutters across the page.

We imagine a place, a moment,
when these appear in your hands
like strange birds, delicate,
weathered from the trip.

They open their small mouths.

Devotion lasts, and it is sung
in the voices of those
who are left behind,
making peace with the incomplete,
inarticulate, half-said.
The past is past and still
we write, fold, send, believe

they arrive in the place
between now and the day
their zig-zag flight mimics
the one we'll take
when we, too, disappear.

Once, a nestling fell
from the rafters of the porch
and lay like a missive
on our front step. Its feathers
spread to reveal the thinnest
layer of bird-skin, pulsing
with tiny veins. Too small

to fly, we put it back in the nest,
up high, with five siblings
who knocked it out again.

Once, it opened its mouth as if
to feed, and what came out
was half breath, half sound,
from some world that wished
to take it back and did,
that day, when its shivering

stilled. We felt culpable.
We had touched it, sullied
the world it fell out of.

These letters feel safe, reach
out to you who we've loved
from this tenuous distance—

draw the flight line between us—

honor the fact that we are still
here with our earthy language
written, folded, sent to you
in ink, on paper, on the wind,

wing-like, into the nest of your palms.

Pedro Serrano & Catalina Fernandez
b. Jerez de Badajoz, Spain, 15th century

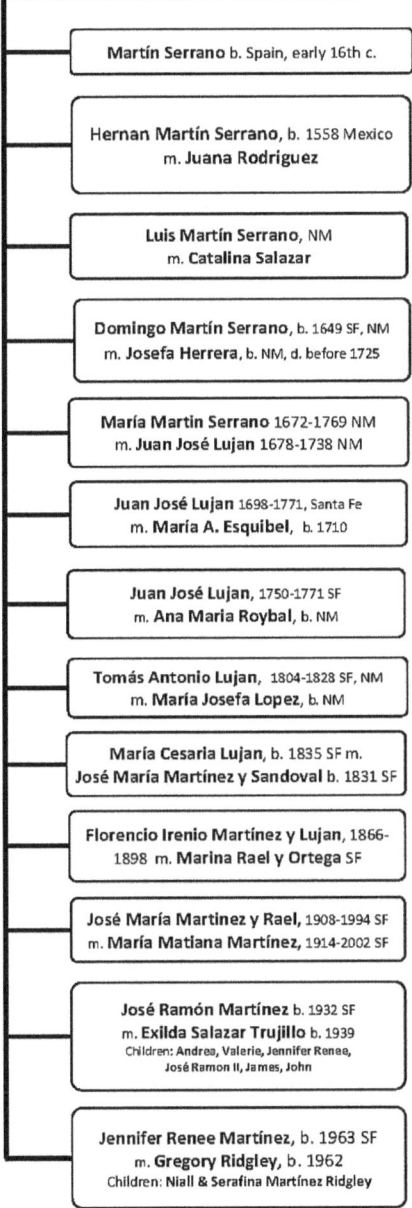

Martín Serrano b. Spain, early 16th c.

Hernan Martín Serrano, b. 1558 Mexico
m. Juana Rodriguez

Luis Martín Serrano, NM
m. Catalina Salazar

Domingo Martín Serrano, b. 1649 SF, NM
m. Josefa Herrera, b. NM, d. before 1725

María Martin Serrano 1672-1769 NM
m. Juan José Lujan 1678-1738 NM

Juan José Lujan 1698-1771, Santa Fe
m. María A. Esquibel, b. 1710

Juan José Lujan, 1750-1771 SF
m. Ana Maria Roybal, b. NM

Tomás Antonio Lujan, 1804-1828 SF, NM
m. María Josefa Lopez, b. NM

María Cesaria Lujan, b. 1835 SF m.
José María Martínez y Sandoval b. 1831 SF

Florencio Irenio Martínez y Lujan, 1866-
1898 m. Marina Rael y Ortega SF

José María Martinez y Rael, 1908-1994 SF
m. María Matiana Martínez, 1914-2002 SF

José Ramón Martínez b. 1932 SF
m. Exilda Salazar Trujillo b. 1939
Children: Andrea, Valerie, Jennifer Renee,
José Ramon II, James, John

Jennifer Renee Martínez, b. 1963 SF
m. Gregory Ridgley, b. 1962
Children: Niall & Serafina Martínez Ridgley

William J. Ridgley Sr., d. 1716 Maryland
m. Elizabeth Clark

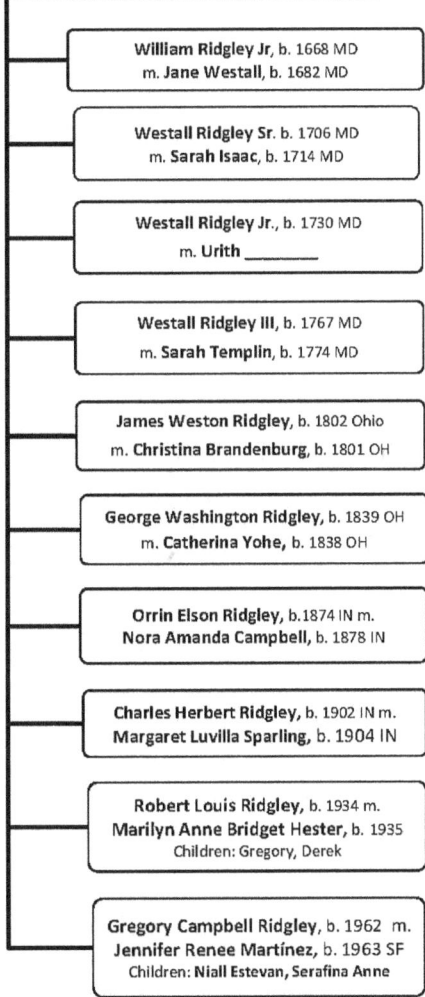

William Ridgley Jr, b. 1668 MD
m. Jane Westall, b. 1682 MD

Westall Ridgley Sr. b. 1706 MD
m. Sarah Isaac, b. 1714 MD

Westall Ridgley Jr., b. 1730 MD
m. Urith _____

Westall Ridgley III, b. 1767 MD
m. Sarah Templin, b. 1774 MD

James Weston Ridgley, b. 1802 Ohio
m. Christina Brandenburg, b. 1801 OH

George Washington Ridgley, b. 1839 OH
m. Catherina Yohe, b. 1838 OH

Orrin Elson Ridgley, b.1874 IN m.
Nora Amanda Campbell, b. 1878 IN

Charles Herbert Ridgley, b. 1902 IN m.
Margaret Luvilla Sparling, b. 1904 IN

Robert Louis Ridgley, b. 1934 m.
Marilyn Anne Bridget Hester, b. 1935
Children: Gregory, Derek

Gregory Campbell Ridgley, b. 1962 m.
Jennifer Renee Martínez, b. 1963 SF
Children: Niall Estevan, Serafina Anne

THE MARTÍNEZ RIDGLEY FAMILY

The Ortiz Dinkel Family

Reynalda Ortiz y Pino

The Ortiz y Pino and Ortiz Dinkel families, about 1950.

The Ortiz Dinkel Family

The Ortiz Dinkel Family

Participating Family Members and Ages

First Generation—Judith Ann Brito Hasted (66), Ronald Eric Ortiz Dinkel (65)
Second Generation—Anne Renee Brito (44), Robert Patrick Brito (40), Elizabeth Aimee Brito Wilkes (37), Michael Aaron Brito (32)
Third Generation—Damien R. Brito (16), Kira Sterling Wilkes (11), Tyler Austin Wilkes (8), Jacob Travis Wilkes (6), Maelynne Rae Brito (3), Liliana Judita Brito (1)

Brief Family History

Thirteen generations of the Ortiz family have lived in New Mexico. Nicolas Ortiz and Mariana Coronado, with their seven children, came to New Mexico as colonists with the de Vargas reconquest of 1693. In Spain, Nicolas Ortiz served in the army and fought in last battle against the Moors. In New Mexico, Nicolas Ortiz II was cited for valor by Don Diego de Vargas for fighting in the battles against the Indians of Taos and Picuris. Nicolas Ortiz III was a lieutenant at the Santa Fe Presidio and died in the Indian campaign near Abiquiu in 1769. His widow was instrumental in reviving the Fiesta de Santa Fe and the Confradia de la Conquistadora.

Antonio José Ortiz, second son of Nicolas Ortiz III and Gertrudis, helped to build and enlarge the Conquistadora chapel after it fell into ruin about 1798. He also restored the ancient church of San Miguel and built Rosario Chapel. Ana María Baca, a daughter of Antonio José Ortiz and Gertrudis, married Don Pedro Bautista Pino. Don Pedro had the distinction of being the first and only deputy from New Mexico to the Spanish Cortes in 1810. Don Pedro's son, Don Nicolas de Jesus Pino, was among those who plotted the overthrow of the newly arrived U. S. government in 1846. Nicolas controlled the vast grazing lands of the Galisteo basin.

Concepcion Pino, daughter of Don Nicolas, married Juan Ortiz, thus bringing back the Ortiz name to the family tree. A descendant of Captain Nicolas Ortiz, Juan's ancestors were given the Ortiz mining grant at the foot of the Ortiz mountains, named for the family. Their children included Pedro Ortiz y Pino, born 1882, father of Reynalda, Virginia, Pedro, and Jose Ortiz y Pino. Jose Ortiz y Pino served as a member of the New Mexico House of Representatives from 1926 until 1928. He was a prominent New Mexican, rancher, and owner of a mercantile in Galisteo. His daughter, Concha, became a state legislator in the 1930's, serving as majority whip, as well as an educator, rancher, and renowned philanthropist in her own right.

Reynalda Ortiz Dinkel (mother of Judy Hasted and Ron Dinkel, grandmother of Anne Brito—participants in the Lines & Circles project) was born on January 11, 1912 as New Mexico became the forty-seventh state of the United States. An educator for more than thirty years, one of the original charter members of La Sociedad Folklorica, Reynalda was La Reina de las Fiestas de Santa Fe in 1938. She was a published poet and author of numerous works. Judith Ann Hasted is Reynalda's daughter and a retired educator, community volunteer, member of La Sociedad Folklorica, and Mayordomo. Ronald Eric Ortiz Dinkel is Reynalda's son and was the Director of Human Resources at the College of Santa Fe. Anne Renee Brito, eldest daughter of Judy, resides in Albuquerque where she is a pharmacy technician.

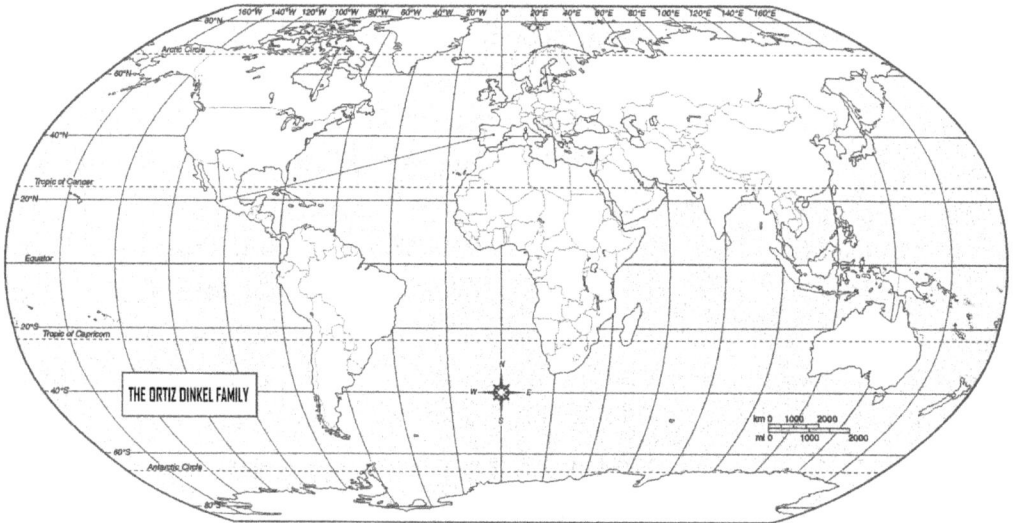

THE ORTIZ DINKEL FAMILY

Family Traditions

Devotions—Las Posadas, Christmas Vigil, sing-alongs in the neighborhood, Midnight Mass, Tres Reyes; Velorio de Santa Ana; *Processions*—Corpus Christi, Fiesta de Santa Fé, Pilgrimage to el Santuario de Chimayo; *Lent*—visitation at the churches on Holy Thursday; *Organizations and Celebrations*—La Sociedad Folklorica, El Rancho de Golondrinas, La Merienda and el Baile de los Cascarones (de la Sociedad Folklorica); *Education*—Loretto Academy and St. Michael's High School, University of New Mexico, New Mexico State University, Eastern New Mexico University, New Mexico State, College of Santa Fe; *Scouting*—Brownie and Girl Scouts, Cub and Boy Scouts.

Family Heirlooms

Rosaries; a trastero (refinished and painted with retablos by Monica Sosaya Halford); a trunk belonging to Juana Rascon; crosses; a pre dieux; dresses belonging to Manuela Pino Sena, Agueda Pino, Virginia Rael, and other members of the Ortiz y Pino families; mantones and shawls; colchas; antique furniture including the family table in our Lines & Circles work of art.

Family Recipes

Mama's red chile; blue corn enchiladas; Nana's empanaditas and sweet tamales; panocha; natillas; posole and chicos quebrados; albondigas; atole; egg nog; torta de huevo with camarones; calabacitas.

What We Love About Santa Fe

Its history, in which our family has played a major role; Santa Fe's architectural wonders; "founding families" of several Santa Feans of diverse ethnic and cultural backgrounds; the unique personalities, past and present, who have contributed to Santa Fe's rich fabric.

What Troubles Us about Our Hometown

Its growth has sacrificed its uniqueness; "Santa Fe Style," which has encouraged homogeneity and discouraged distinct cultural expressions; everything is behind adobe walls, no openness.

The Ortiz Dinkel Family Today

The Family Table
by
Ronald Ortiz Dinkel

What is this table?
Wrought from what fine, incorruptible oak,
Circular and satinized by the touch of years.
The years do not disappear into forgetfulness.
What has been lived remains like a sentinel
Observing an endless conversation.
One strong symbol of the value of succession in life.
Forged from constancy,
Formed from loyalty;
Remembrances of how they were and we now are
Surround me.
Each one had his dreams and ambitions.
Each one had her own thoughts and aspirations.
Each faces life following the dictates of his own heart,
An ever-binding thread of acceptance
Through family members sharing appealing food,
Engaging in enjoyable conversation,
Teaching values and nurturing familial relationships.

La Mesa de Familia

¿Cuál es esta mesa?
Forjado de que roble fino, incorruptible,
Circular y limpiada por el toque de años.
Los años no desaparecen en el olvido.
Lo que ha sido vivido permanece como una centinela
Que observa una conversación interminable.
Un símbolo fuerte del valor de sucesión en vida.
Forjado de constancia,
Formado de lealtad;

Los recuerdos de como ellos eran y ahora nosotros estamos
Rodéeme.
Cada uno tenía sus sueños y ambiciones.
Cada uno tenía sus propios pensamientos y aspiraciones.
Cada afronte la vida con los mandatos de su propio corazón,
Un hilo siempre-obligatorio de aceptación
Por miembros de familia que comparten alimento sabroso,
Conversación agradable,
Enseñando de valores y nutriendo relaciones de familia.

(Translation by Valerie Martínez)

THE ORTIZ Y PINO FAMILY

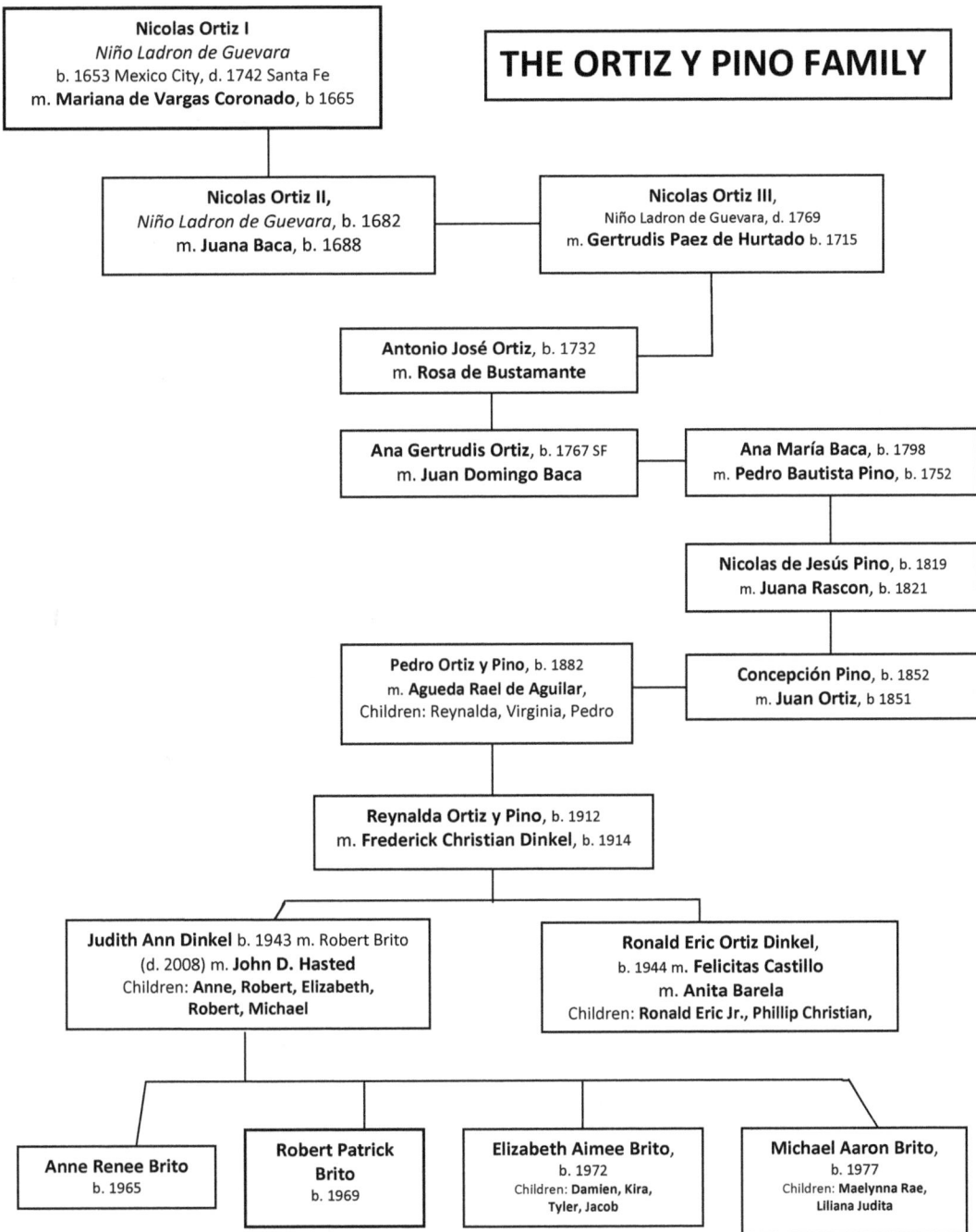

Nicolas Ortiz I
Niño Ladron de Guevara
b. 1653 Mexico City, d. 1742 Santa Fe
m. **Mariana de Vargas Coronado**, b 1665

Nicolas Ortiz II,
Niño Ladron de Guevara, b. 1682
m. **Juana Baca**, b. 1688

Nicolas Ortiz III,
Niño Ladron de Guevara, d. 1769
m. **Gertrudis Paez de Hurtado** b. 1715

Antonio José Ortiz, b. 1732
m. **Rosa de Bustamante**

Ana Gertrudis Ortiz, b. 1767 SF
m. **Juan Domingo Baca**

Ana María Baca, b. 1798
m. **Pedro Bautista Pino**, b. 1752

Nicolas de Jesús Pino, b. 1819
m. **Juana Rascon**, b. 1821

Pedro Ortiz y Pino, b. 1882
m. **Agueda Rael de Aguilar**,
Children: Reynalda, Virginia, Pedro

Concepción Pino, b. 1852
m. **Juan Ortiz**, b 1851

Reynalda Ortiz y Pino, b. 1912
m. **Frederick Christian Dinkel**, b. 1914

Judith Ann Dinkel b. 1943 m. Robert Brito
(d. 2008) m. **John D. Hasted**
Children: **Anne, Robert, Elizabeth,
Robert, Michael**

Ronald Eric Ortiz Dinkel,
b. 1944 m. **Felicitas Castillo**
m. **Anita Barela**
Children: **Ronald Eric Jr., Phillip Christian,**

Anne Renee Brito
b. 1965

**Robert Patrick
Brito**
b. 1969

Elizabeth Aimee Brito,
b. 1972
Children: **Damien, Kira,
Tyler, Jacob**

Michael Aaron Brito,
b. 1977
Children: **Maelynna Rae,
Liliana Judita**

The Quintana Gallegos Family

Celestine and Joe Quintana, Palm Springs 1943.

The Quintana Gallegos Family

The Quintana Gallegos Family

Participating Family Members and Ages

First Generation—Celestine G. Quintana Draves (*in memoriam*)

Second Generation—Roberta "Bobbi" Quintana Gallegos (71)

Third Generation—Carla Gallegos Parker (46), Roberta Gallegos-Siller (44), Paula Gallegos Reynolds (40)

Fourth Generation: Ashley (22), Stephanie (21), Emma (18), David (15), Bethany (10), Saige (9)

Brief Family History
by Bobbi Gallegos

My maternal grandparents, Pelagia Baca Gonzales and Suncion Gonzales, were born in 1898 and 1897, respectively, in Santa Rosa, New Mexico. Both she and my grandfather were teachers. My grandfather was elected to the New Mexico Legislature representing Guadalupe County. After his term of office was over, he chose to remain in Santa Fe. Pelagio and Suncion had two daughters, Celestine (my mother) and Pearla, born in Santa Rosa in 1915 and 1917. After they moved to Santa Fe, they attended and graduated from Loretto Academy in 1933 and 1935. My mother continued her education by taking business courses. She retired from the New Mexico Supreme Court where she served as secretary to Chief Justices Sadler, Moise, McManus and McKenna. She died in 2005 after a brief illness.

My paternal grandparents, Alejandro and Josefita Quintana, were born and raised in Santa Fe. My grandfather owned a grocery store on Agua Fria Street. He was also a jeweler specializing in gold filigree. My father was the 6th of their twelve children. My father attended local public schools, graduating in 1935 with letters in football, basketball and track. Right after high school he began taking flying lessons and received his pilot's license. In 1937, he joined the New Mexico state police and in 1942 became a civilian flying instructor for the Army. A year later, having received his commission, he was sent to the Ferry Command at Long Beach, California, and later to the 21st Ferrying Group at Palm Springs. In November of 1943 he left the United States for overseas duty. After a brief training course in England, he joined the Air Service Command. On March 21, 1944, my father was returning to his base in Kidlington, England on a very foggy day when he crashed into a tree and was killed instantly.

As a result of my father's service, I was one of the first New Mexico students to apply for and receive college funds under the War Orphan Act. I attended the University of New Mexico, graduating in 1958 with a Bachelor of Science in Education. I married Henry L. Gallegos on August 23, 1958. We were blessed with five children: David Gregory, Carla Jo, Roberta Lee, Michael Henry, and Paula Christine.

Greg is employed by the Bureau of Land Management as an Information Technology Specialist. His children, Emma Celeste and David Gregory, attend Santa Fe High School. Carla is the office manager for Dowlen Sound in Denver and an exercise instructor at the Denver Athletic Club. Her daughter, Ashley, is an aspiring model, currently working and residing in Aspen. Roberta is employed in Austin as an Administrative Assistant to the Texas Facilities Commission. Their children, Stephanie and Steven, are college students. Michael has a dental practice in Santa Fe where he resides with his wife Jolene and their three children, Alex, Bethany and Saige. Paula is a licensed Massage Therapist and Pilates instructor. She is employed as Spa Director at the Farmhouse Inn in Forestville, California, and is also proprietor of a private Pilates and Massage studio, *Wholistic Balance*.

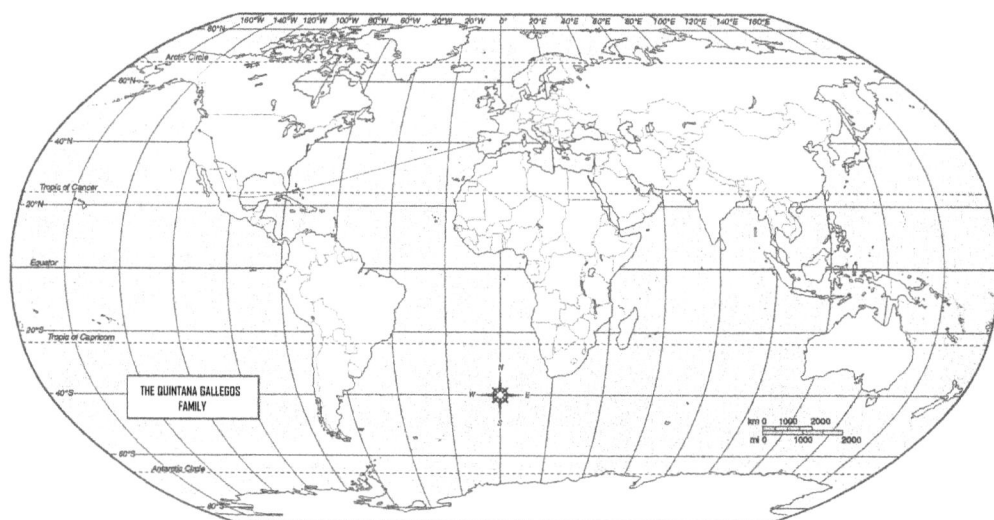

THE QUINTANA GALLEGOS FAMILY

Family Traditions

We have always celebrated baptisms, First Holy Communions, Confirmations, birthdays, graduations, and the important holidays of Easter, July 4th, Thanksgiving, and Christmas. We come together at funerals. We also get together to make tamales, empanaditas, divinity and other foods handed down by previous generations. Bobbi learned to sew from her paternal grandmother (Josefita Maes Quintana) and mother (Celestine). Her maternal grandmother taught her to crochet afghans. One of Bobbi's grand aunts (Josefita Quintana Pettine) taught her to tat lace. Quilting was taught to Celestine by her aunt Sinforiana Baca Lucero. The quilt for the *Lines & Circles* project was begun by Bobbi's mother on the day the astronauts first landed on the moon. Bobbi's mom later taught her the intricacies of quilting and she has now passed on the craft to her daughters and granddaughters.

Family Heirlooms

Gold filigree jewelry, a silver belt with the initials RQ (for Bobbi), a ruby ring—all made by Bobbi's paternal grandfather. Celestine made Bobbi's First Communion dress from her husband's silk parachute. She also made Bobbi's wedding dress and, later, from the same material, made the baptismal gown that each of her grandchildren wore when they were baptized in the Catholic Church.

Family Recipes

Bobbi's paternal grandmother made delicious Lemon and Pineapple Pies, an Apricot Spice Cake, a Potato Devil's-Food Cake. Her paternal grandfather owned a grocery store and, on a whim, would bring home watermelon to make homemade watermelon ice cream.

What We Love About Santa Fe

The architecture, culture, our traditions, including the patchwork of people.

Changes We'd Like To See

We are dismayed at the increase of crime in our city. Though change is inevitable, we are not the close-knit community we once were. We need to get more of the old Santa Fe families to participate in community gatherings.

The Quintana Gallegos Family

The Quintana Gallegos Quilt
by
Valerie Martínez

The day we landed on the moon,
July 20, 1969, she began:
remnants of fabric—
white, pale pink, patterned—
      cut and folded and pieced,
      mapped out on the same table
      where the family talked and ate.
      Stitch by stitch, she started a quilt,
something like the patchwork
seen by astronauts hurling
back to earth—Midwest
fields and farms from outer space.
      It reminded them
      of the past, grandmothers,
      mothers and sisters
      at the hearth, the fabric
between them, the sounds
of laughter and chatter.
It made them yearn;
it made them dream of home.

Celestine Quintana learned
to quilt from her aunt,
María Sinforiana Baca,
born 1902. She passed it on,
the stitching, the circular motion,
      of needle in hand
      to her daughter, Bobbi,
      who in turn teaches it
      to her girls—

Carla, Roberta, Paula—
who pass it down to theirs—
Emma, Ashley, Stephanie,
Bethany, and Saige.
        The quilt is a map
        of the past and present,
        commonly held,
        bound by these threads
between fingers
with similar shapes,
also passed down
from generation to generation.

        What is precious is held
        then descends through time—
        quilts, ruby rings, gold filigree,
        a silver belt buckle with "RQ"
given to Bobbi by her grandfather,
a grocer and jeweler, with his love.
This quilt, these heirlooms tether us
to each other and who we are,
        remind us that no matter how far
        away, from here to outer space
        or eternity, our loved ones are as close
        as what remains here, in our loving hands.

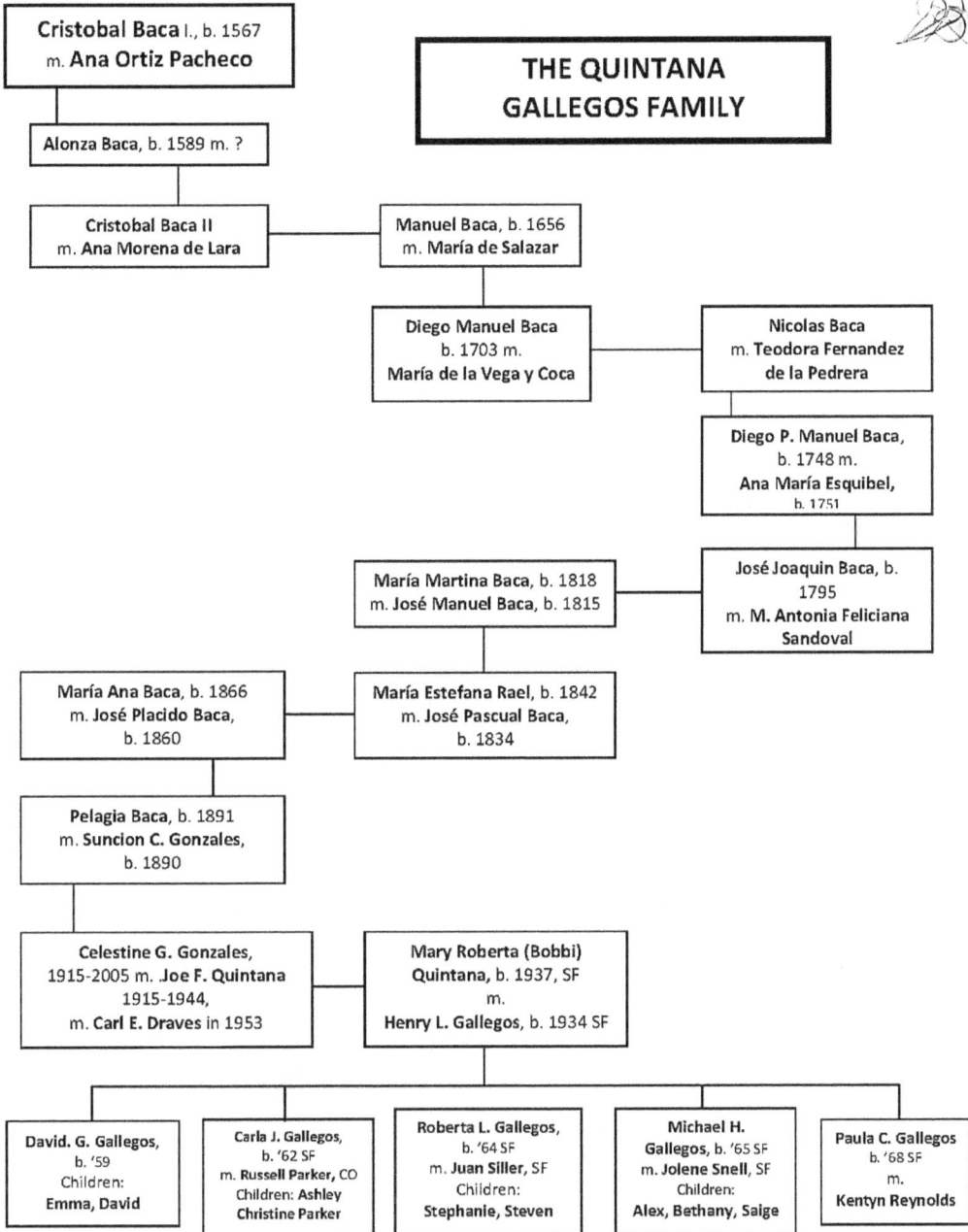

Cristobal Baca I., b. 1567
m. **Ana Ortiz Pacheco**

Alonza Baca, b. 1589 m. ?

Cristobal Baca II
m. **Ana Morena de Lara**

Manuel Baca, b. 1656
m. **María de Salazar**

Diego Manuel Baca
b. 1703 m.
María de la Vega y Coca

Nicolas Baca
m. **Teodora Fernandez
de la Pedrera**

Diego P. Manuel Baca,
b. 1748 m.
Ana María Esquibel,
b. 1751

María Martina Baca, b. 1818
m. **José Manuel Baca**, b. 1815

José Joaquin Baca, b.
1795
m. **M. Antonia Feliciana
Sandoval**

María Ana Baca, b. 1866
m. **José Placido Baca,**
b. 1860

María Estefana Rael, b. 1842
m. **José Pascual Baca,**
b. 1834

Pelagia Baca, b. 1891
m. **Suncion C. Gonzales,**
b. 1890

Celestine G. Gonzales,
1915-2005 m. .**Joe F. Quintana**
1915-1944,
m. **Carl E. Draves** in 1953

Mary Roberta (Bobbi)
Quintana, b. 1937, SF
m.
Henry L. Gallegos, b. 1934 SF

David. G. Gallegos,
b. '59
Children:
Emma, David

Carla J. Gallegos,
b. '62 SF
m. **Russell Parker,** CO
Children: **Ashley
Christine Parker**

Roberta L. Gallegos,
b. '64 SF
m. **Juan Siller,** SF
Children:
Stephanie, Steven

Michael H.
Gallegos, b. '65 SF
m. **Jolene Snell,** SF
Children:
Alex, Bethany, Saige

Paula C. Gallegos
b. '68 SF
m.
Kentyn Reynolds

The
Salazar
Family

Julia and Dennis Salazar, 1965

The Salazar Family

The Salazar Family

Participating Family Members and Ages

First Generation—Cleofas Vigil (86)

Second Generation—Julia Salazar (65)

Third Generation—Dennis L. Salazar (40), Carl Salazar (43),

Fourth Generation—Nic Salazar (22), Sarah Salazar (18), Gabriela Salazar (14), Jack Salazar (8)

Brief Family History
by Julia Salazar

The surname "Salazar" is an ancient name which originated in Portugal and Vizcaya, Castile, Navarre, Santander, and Burgos, Spain. The name means "one who came from Salazar (the manor house in Spain), dweller in or near the house or palace; dweller near the place sacred to St. Lazar (1329-1389)." Other variations include "Salzar" and "Salazaro."

As the Salazar population grew, they settled in Northern New Mexico as well as in the San Luis Valley in Colorado. A prominent member of the Salazar family was Manuel Sabino Salazar of Abiquiu, New Mexico (1833-1879) who was appointed Postmaster of Rio Arriba County in 1865 by President Abraham Lincoln. My husband Dennis Salazar's parents, Joaquin Salazar and Odila Lucero, brought up their nine children in Hernandez and in Santa Fe. Dennis remembers his parents always working hard and losing his mother to illness at a very young age. His father believed education and religion were very important. The Salazar children grew up in a strict home, attending Catholic school, attending church often, and working at early ages.

My parents, Cleofas Vigil and Merejildo Roybal, raised their four children in Santa Fe and Pecos. Merejildo was a Penitente in Pecos, and the family participated in the moradas, rosaries, and velorios. My father was the spiritual leader of the family and community. He engaged in long discussions of theology and the Bible with friends. My mother was a homemaker and canned fruit and vegetables—chile, tamales, and capulin jam. She still works hard, (at 86 years old), making bread and tortillas for her family and charities. Both my mother and I belong to the Union Protectiva Femenina.

Donaciano Vigil of Santa Fe and Pecos (1802-1877), an ancestor in the Vigil family, served as territorial governor of New Mexico in the transitional period from 1847 to 1848. Vigil was also, a soldier, legislator and founder of the Santa Fe newspaper, *La Verdad* (1844).

Military service is an important tradition in the Salazar and Vigil families. Ancestors were soldiers in the armies of the Spanish Conquest and navy men during World War II and the Cold War. Carl and Dennis Lloyd Salazar, ours sons, served in the Persian Gulf and Saudi Arabia during Desert Storm. It was stressful having both sons, our only children, at war at the same time. The family is proud of military service and loyalty to the country.

Today, the Salazar family lives in Santa Fe and Houston. We remain close through telephone and email and we get together for holidays and other important occasions. The Salazar families talk a lot about their upbringing, morality, and God. We remind our children and grandchildren about responsibilities and the importance of reaching goals and dreams. We support each other and listen to our sons and grandchildren. Our opinions are still valued by our sons. We talk about worship and the importance of communication with God. We remind them that God has a sense of humor.

The Salazar family considers living in Santa Fe a special privilege.

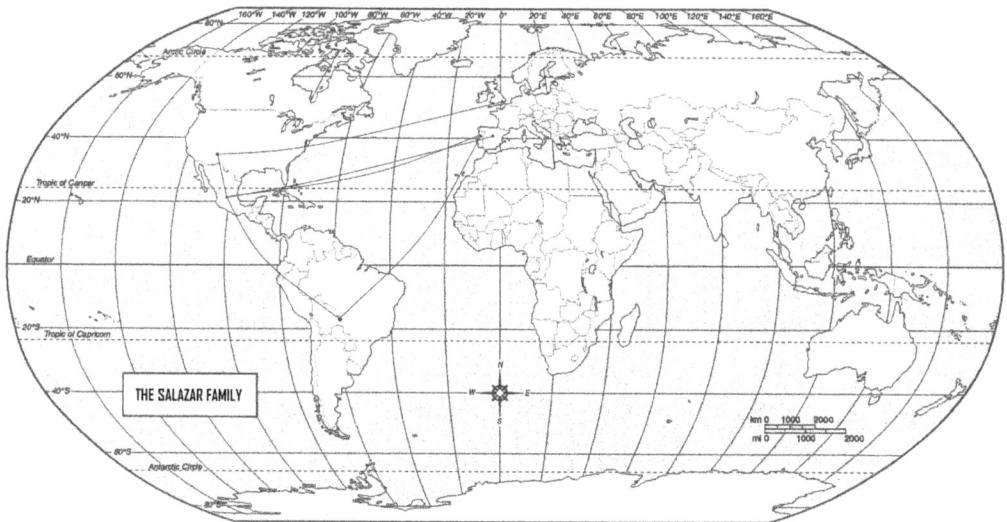

THE SALAZAR FAMILY

Family Traditions

Penitente gatherings; sheep and goat raising; cheese-making; ground pit meat (cabrito) roasting, adobe building.

Family Heirlooms

A ceramic altar, knick-knacks trunk, Joaquin Salazar's Bible, a shawl woven by Julia's grandfather.

Family Recipes

Bread pudding; capulin jelly; homemade bread; chili stew; red chile sauce.

What We Love About Santa Fe

The mountains, sunsets, weather, rich history, cultures, diversity.

What Troubles us About Our Hometown

Non-affordable housing; limited downtown parking; lack of water resources; downtown retailers have had to move elsewhere due to high rents; beautification and improvement seem to happen only where tourists visit; the rest of the city deserves more attention, including street repair and removal of graffiti on walls.

Nicolas Salazar

The Salazar family today (minus Nicolas)

As Time Goes By
by Julia Salazar

The echoes of the Sangre de Cristo mountains
must call your name, for it is said
that in a time of uncertainty,
you rode into this strange land
we would one day call home.

Dressed in suits of armor, you arrived
ready to conquer promised lands.
You proceeded, not knowing the challenges
and what lay in these vast open spaces.

How, you must have missed your own land
and those loved ones left behind.
Your faith in God, your hopes and dreams
drove you to continue on this long and difficult journey.

The stories have left us with appreciation
for your great hardships and with some pleasure
in the ownership of some of the things you dreamed.

Today we still honor a great lady
that journeyed with you. She came to be known
as the Queen of Peace or La Conquistadora,
and is very famous. Her home
is one of the grandest churches of New Mexico,
the Cathedral Basilica of Saint Francis Of Assisi.
La Conquistadora is very much a part
of our city's celebrations and religious novenas.
She holds a special place in the hearts
of New Mexico's people. She is visited
and greatly admired by people the world over.

So it came to be that your arrival
would make a mark in history.

The promised land became your home
and eventually it became our home.
The land you once struggled to reach
became rich with culture, families, homes and farms,
with churches, moradas, schoolhouses and businesses.

As time passed, some family members
took up sheep raising and became weavers,
others farmed wheat and built flourmills.
Some of our family members became governing figures,
lawmakers and educators and postmasters,
while others became homemakers and midwives.
Some chose to seek their fortune in mineral mining
and set out to distant places to seek their wealth.

The story goes that for some fortune hunters
this craze ended and laying rail for rapid transit
made more profit. Carpentry and stone masonry
also became necessary trades. People built homes
and other structures out of stone, mud and adobe
but eventually they thought of using wood lumber
as this method of building was quicker.

Soon sawmills and concrete plants made the scene.
As cities grew larger, our forests grew smaller.
As generations have come and gone,
most every generation has had loved ones
go to wars in foreign lands. Some gave up their lives
fighting for our freedom, and others came back as heroes.

Family gatherings celebrating happy occasions
as well as sad ones continue in our towns.
Church gatherings are still celebrated with prayer
and music and, depending on the holiday,
with processions. Weddings, baptisms and funerals
are still the main reasons for families coming together.

As time passes, we continue to learn about you,
who you were and who we are.
We continue to grow as a family and as a nation.
Modern technology plays an important role
in our daily lives. Some of us struggle with this
and the speed of modern-time events.

And so, some of us adjust to these times
while others struggle and recall old ways.
And every time another elder passes on
we recall the good old days, as we stand still
and watch more time go by.

THE SALAZAR FAMILY

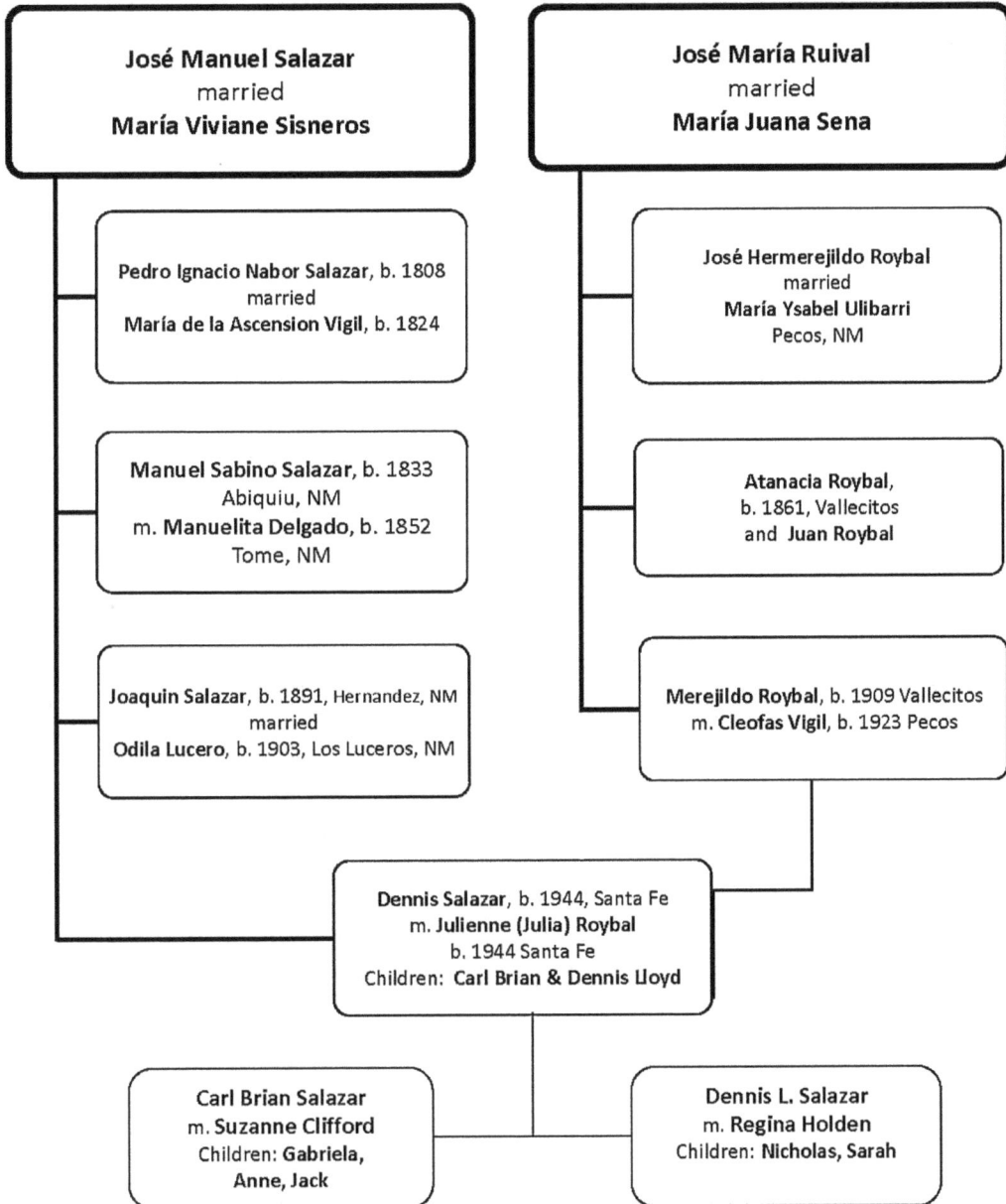

José Manuel Salazar
married
María Viviane Sisneros

José María Ruival
married
María Juana Sena

Pedro Ignacio Nabor Salazar, b. 1808
married
María de la Ascension Vigil, b. 1824

José Hermerejildo Roybal
married
María Ysabel Ulibarri
Pecos, NM

Manuel Sabino Salazar, b. 1833
Abiquiu, NM
m. **Manuelita Delgado**, b. 1852
Tome, NM

Atanacia Roybal,
b. 1861, Vallecitos
and Juan Roybal

Joaquin Salazar, b. 1891, Hernandez, NM
married
Odila Lucero, b. 1903, Los Luceros, NM

Merejildo Roybal, b. 1909 Vallecitos
m. **Cleofas Vigil**, b. 1923 Pecos

Dennis Salazar, b. 1944, Santa Fe
m. **Julienne (Julia) Roybal**
b. 1944 Santa Fe
Children: **Carl Brian & Dennis Lloyd**

Carl Brian Salazar
m. **Suzanne Clifford**
Children: **Gabriela,
Anne, Jack**

Dennis L. Salazar
m. **Regina Holden**
Children: **Nicholas, Sarah**

The Strongheart Family

The Strongheart Family

Participating Family Members and Ages

First Generation—Paula Strongheart

Second Generation—Lake Strongheart McTighe (38), Faith Laimböck Strongheart (36), Mercy Strongheart Pozgay (34), Lulu Strongheart (33), Dependable Hickory Strongheart (31), Sara Beth Aurelia Star Strongheart Valdez (28)

Third Generation—Isabel Strongheart McTighe (10, daughter of Lake), Zia Lumina del Monte Sol Hicouri Strongheart (8, daughter of Dependable), Vicente Amadeo (2) and Marie Valentina (1) Valdez (children of Sara)

Brief Family History

Paula Strongheart was born with the surname Johnson and grew up in an affluent family that traveled and lived in Afghanistan, France, eastern Canada and Virginia, following her father's career as a diplomat. At 16 she left the dysfunction and abuse of her birth family and fled to New York where she worked as an actor as well as a back-up vocalist (for Stephen Stills, the Carradine brothers, and others). She appeared in the 1967 version of "Hair" on Broadway. Paula divided her time between L.A. and New York with acting and singing gigs and life was busy and wild in the midst of the 60's and 70's hippie movement.

In the late 60's, with the cast of the film "The Good Guys and the Bad Guys" (starring Robert Mitchum and George Kennedy) she traveled to Chama, New Mexico for filming. She fell in love with New Mexico from the moment her plane landed at the Santa Fe airport. While in New Mexico, Paula became pregnant with her first child, Lake, and decided to stay for good. She changed her name to Strongheart, based on her spiritual beliefs, and started a family.

Paula gave each of her children their own last names—(Lake) *Manyfeathers*, (Faith) *Brings the Wild*, (Mercy) *Blue Sky that Never Darkens*, (Hallelujah "Lulu") *Mist on the Mountains*, (Dependable) *Hickory*, and (Sara Beth Aurelia) *Star*. One family story explains the origins of her son Dependable Hickory's name. Michael, his father, was a woodcutter while he and Paula pursued their "Back-To-The-Land" dreams in the '70's. Michael chopped trees by hand and his ax handles would frequently break. One day, fed up, he invested in an expensive axe handle made of hickory. It had the words "Dependable Hickory" carved into it. Lo and behold, the handle didn't break. Leaning against his truck one day, taking a break from chopping, he said to Paula, "If I ever have a son I'm going to name him 'Dependable Hickory.' Either that or 'P.M. Breezes.'"

The extended Strongheart family (including spouses, partners, and three grandchildren) descends from Cree Indians and European immigrants from Sweden, Ireland, Scotland, France, and Russia. Family members practice a range of non-European religions including Shambala Buddhist, Pagan Spiritual, Sun Worshipper, and the Native American Church.

Music-making is at the center of Strongheart family life, descending from Paula (whose rock ballads were the mainstay of her early career) and including many of her children. Music has always been a powerful force the binds together family members. Family members play and celebrate the traditional music of northern New Mexico as well as music from all over the world. Music has kept parents, children, siblings, nieces and nephews and grandchildren close.

Strongheart family members are also students, urban planners, filmmakers, polarity therapists, massage therapists, DJ's, teachers, contruction workers, estheticians and IT managers. The Stronghearts greatest hope for their family is to cultivate their own family traditions that will keep family members safe, happy and thriving and pass down to many new generations.

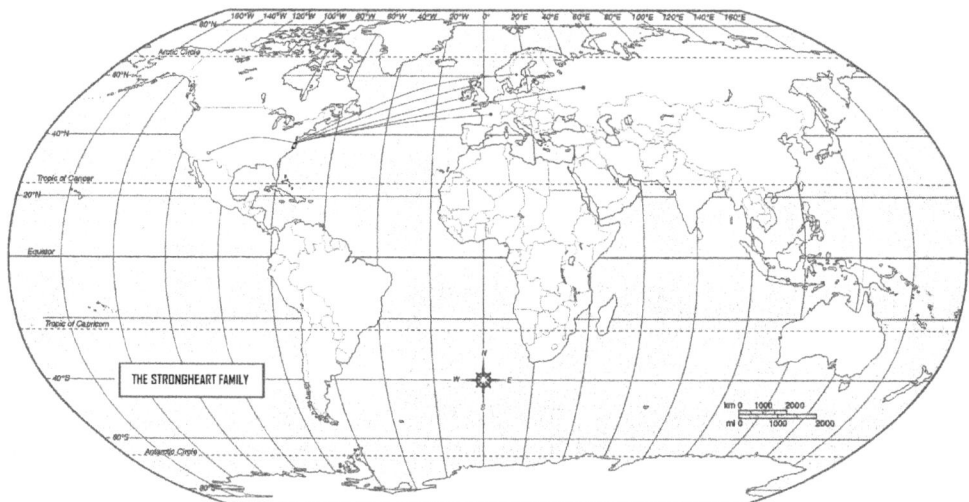

THE STRONGHEART FAMILY

Family Traditions

Getting together for Christmas, Thanksgiving, weddings, summer vacations, funerals. We usually participate in a variety of activities including playing music, eating, being outdoors and sharing conversation. Family gatherings are large and wonderful.

Family Recipes
Pasta Dishes, Cinnamon Kuchen, Turkey and Stuffing, Swedish Meatballs, Beef Stroganoff.

What We Love About Santa Fe
The food, Christmas-time, the landscape, the climate, the sky, mixed cultures, and the quaint architecture.

What Troubles us About Our Hometown
The limited water supply; wealthy part-time residents who do not become part of the day-to-day community; sky-rocketing property values (and the lack of affordable housing); drunk driving rates; rape rates, a poor public school system. The city often seems to cater to tourists as a priority over community members.

Strength and Wisdom

STRONGHEART

Strongheart
by Valerie Martínez

She named them

Lake Manyfeathers,
Faith Brings the Wild,
Mercy Blue Sky That Never Darkens

wishing them fortitude, grace,
wisdom, the compassion

to carry them through the days
and into their dreams.

In the 70's, Paula in long hair,
beads, flowers and fringe
left the past, took a new name,
and came west.

She put down
roots in this place,
mothered six
she called

Halleluiah Mist on the Mountains,
Dependable Hickory,
Sarah Beth Aurelia Star.

From one to fourteen
the Strongheart extended family

fills many homes, theirs
and ours, with music—

traditional (hear the songs
of northern New Mexico)—
and tunes all their own.

The Strongheart hands
also work buildings, bodies,
turntables; they plan cities,
make movies, hit the books
and teach on blackboards.

They change where we live.

Isabel, Frans, Stephen, Daniel,
Zia Lumina del Monte Sol.

For one and fourteen
the Strongheart
Coat of Arms claims

Compassion
Love
Forgiveness
Trust

with a winged heart,
sun-sign,
four bound arrows
and a horse whose hoofs
never touch the ground.

Vicente Amadeo,
Marie Valentina.

Winged Family,
Family of the Sun
and Four Directions,
Family that Flies
Lightly Over the Earth

with a Strong Heart.

THE STRONGHEART FAMILY

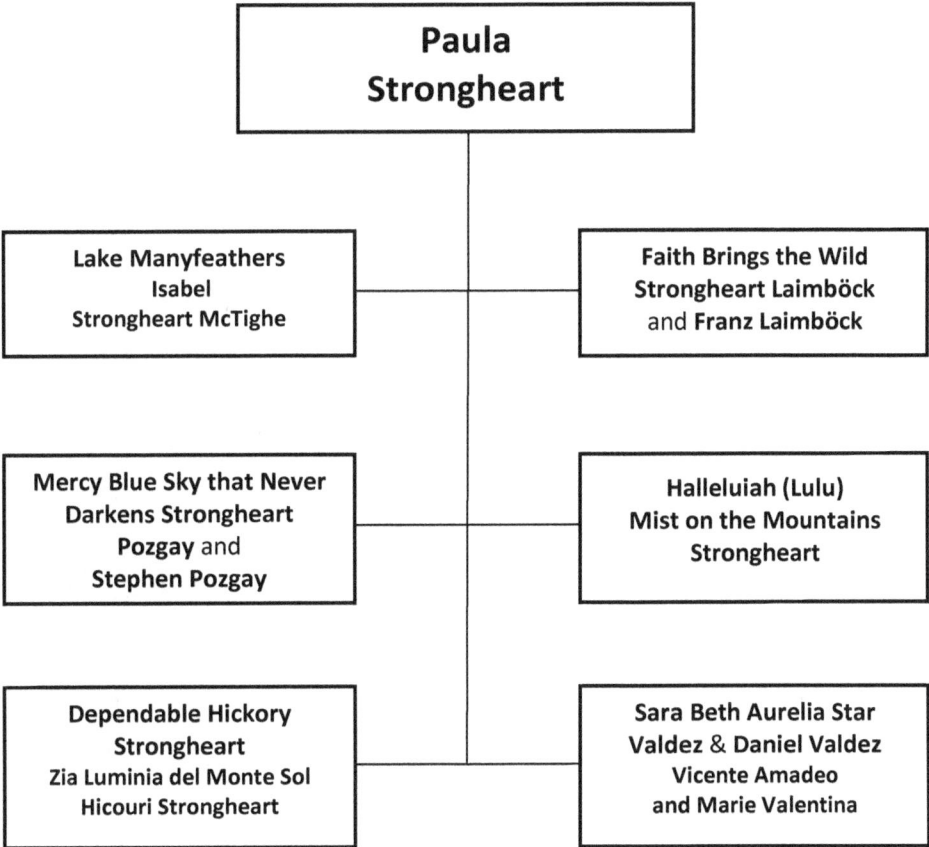

Paula Strongheart

Lake Manyfeathers
Isabel
Strongheart McTighe

Faith Brings the Wild
Strongheart Laimböck
and **Franz Laimböck**

Mercy Blue Sky that Never
Darkens Strongheart
Pozgay and
Stephen Pozgay

Halleluiah (Lulu)
Mist on the Mountains
Strongheart

Dependable Hickory
Strongheart
Zia Luminia del Monte Sol
Hicouri Strongheart

Sara Beth Aurelia Star
Valdez & Daniel Valdez
Vicente Amadeo
and Marie Valentina

Valerie Martínez, Lines and Circles Project Director

alerie Martínez is a poet, teacher, translator, playwright/librettist, editor, and collaborative artist. Her books include *Absence, Luminescent* (Four Way Books), *World to World* and *Each and Her* (University of Arizona Press), *A Flock of Scarlet Doves: Selected Translations of Delmira Agustini* (Sutton Hoo Press), *Reinventing the Enemy's Language* (Norton 1997), and a volume of Santa Fe poems entitled *And They Called it Horizon* (Sunstone Press). Selected Santa Fe poems also appear in a hand-press special collection created by the Palace Press. Valerie is Executive Director of *Littleglobe, Inc*, an artist-run non-profit that collaborates with diverse communities on large-scale art and community dialogue projects. She has a B.A. from Vassar College and an M.F.A. from The University of Arizona. She has taught at the University of Arizona, Ursinus College, New Mexico Highlands University, University of New Mexico, College of Santa Fe and in the rural schools of Swaziland. She is the Poet Laureate for the City of Santa Fe for 2008–2010.

Ilana Kirschbaum, Logo Artist

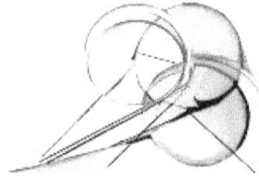

*I*lana Kirschbaum is a visual artist, scenic artist, and designer based in Santa Fe. She is a member of *Theaterwork*, a Santa Fe theater company and has created sets for over 15 productions. During the summer of 2009 she worked in the scenic paint department at the Santa Fe Opera. Recent projects include the set for the world premiere of a Lewis Carol puppet opera and presentation of her own installation entitled "Democracy in America" at the Center for Contemporary Arts. Ilana has worked as a visual artist for the Santa Fe Opera's *Lifesongs* project and is an intern with Littleglobe, a collaborative arts non-profit. Upcoming projects include participation in Chris Jonas' "Garden" project, a multi-media music performance piece. Ilana received a B.A in Liberal Arts from St. John's College in Santa Fe.